An Anthology of Mystery, Menace and Mayhem

Volume I

by

James Ladds

Copyright © James Ladds 2023
All rights reserved in all media. No part of this publication may be reproduced, stored in retrieval system, copied in any form or by any means, electronic, mechanical, photocopying, recording or otherwise transmitted without written permission from the author and/or publisher. You must not circulate this book in any format. Any person who does any unauthorised act in relation to this publication may be liable to criminal prosecution and civil claims for damages.

This novel is a work of fiction. Names, characters, businesses, places, events and incidents are either the products of the author's imagination or used in a fictitious manner. Any resemblance to actual persons, living or dead, or actual events is purely coincidental.

ISBN 978-1-7392438-0-7

For permission requests, please contact:
Jamesladds22@outlook.com

Produced in United Kingdom.

Editorial services by www.bookeditingservices.co.uk

Special thanks to Elaine Strowger, Sue Mackinnon and Debz Hobbs-Wyatt.

Contents

Slamming Doors 5
DNA 28
Leo 62
Trapped 79
Breakdown 101
Restitution 120
Out of Time 140
The Disturbance 167
The Hex 191
Jet 211
The Bus Shelter 225
Ink Blot 238

Slamming Doors

There is an old saying that a "slamming door" is believed to catch the Genius Loci, more commonly known as the "Spirit of Place" which frequents your home. Should this happen, then great misfortune will follow.

The Versants lived in a typical mid-Victorian terrace in Northamptonshire. It was their first home together when they'd married in the late seventies. They had wanted to move, but both lost their jobs during the recession of the nineties, so thought it wise not to add more debt to their mortgage. Even though friends and many of their neighbours were more socially mobile and had moved on, they were content and had settled into a routine.

Cole looked after the back garden, planting bedding plants along the narrow lawn which he mowed each Saturday during the summer. Mika tended the window boxes at the front of the house, which sat securely bolted under each of the sash windows. She also experimented and attempted to trail an English honeysuckle over the front door, but it disappeared along with the wooden planter within a few days. Cole thought it was a blessing, as he was the one who was responsible for pruning, and he could focus on his project for the back garden. He had used railway sleepers to act as steps and bamboo bushes to add height to the low walls.

Over the years, the bushes merged with the little copse at the end of their garden. They were lucky living in an end terrace because it was peaceful. Their only immediate neighbour was an elderly lady called Miss Hartwood. No one ever referred to her by her

Christian name, and Cole would step over the wall and hand her a roast dinner every Sunday.

Miss Hartwood had lived in the same house all her life. Her father's family lived there previously as they ran a greengrocers along Watling Street, where Miss Hartwood worked until her retirement in the 1980s. Her two sisters had long since died and she had few relatives or friends, but she kept herself busy. Her house was spotless and remained unchanged, despite the fashions of neighbouring properties.

Her home stood out from the others as it still had the original wooden single-paned sash windows, and a stained glass front door with the name Villa Rustica above. There was no aerial or satellite dish as Miss Hartwood only listened to the radio.

Miss Hartwood was a stickler for routine. Monday was washday. She'd wheel out an antiquated washing machine from the larder. It was a temperamental contraption, which would often overheat, causing suds and water to overflow onto the floor. Cole attempted to fix it, patching it up here and there, but over time it became more difficult as the parts were long since obsolete. He'd suggested she buy a new modern machine which would be more reliable. She wouldn't hear of it, waving her hand in contempt at such a suggestion.

Tuesday was her day for cleaning, and she'd go around dusting, sweeping the floor, and wiping down the window ledges, corbeils and skirting boards. She'd clean out the fire grate and carry coal up from the cellar, which she had delivered through a hatch at the front of the house below the bay window every October. Her cellar was dark and damp, with the sides of the walls smeared in anthracite. The rest of the street had converted their cellars, passing them off as family rooms.

Wednesday was her shopping day and when venturing out, Miss Hartwood would wear floppy hats, a shawl and wellington boots as she busied herself. She had many idiosyncrasies, including keeping a tray of earth by the back door in which she would step into with her bare feet each day, as she considered it vitally important that you connect with the earth. She bathed in Epsom salts because she considered this removed any negativity from the day, and she was strict on whom she allowed into the house – she didn't want others to leave bad energy in her home. And some nights, if you listened carefully, you could hear Miss Hartwood singing, along with a tinkering of bells.

Thursday and Friday were allocated to tending to her garden. It was a labour of love. She had a mature garden designed by her father, and it contained every variety of fruit tree you could imagine. She had rows upon rows of raspberry canes and other soft fruit. There would always be something to do, such as pruning, repotting, thinning out, raking, hoeing, and deadheading roses and other flowers.

Saturday was her day for visiting the library. She loved reading and would spend hours carefully selecting books. She often read historical novels as well as books on philosophy and religion, and was a keen follower of Helena Blavatsky and George Gurdjieff.

Sunday was observed for exploring. She'd head out early no matter the weather to a park, local historical sites of interest, or she may even drop into a church, museum or local community centre. Miss Hartwood was a keen observer. She'd jot down her observations, and carried a sketch pad to draw and paint in watercolour to capture the events of that day.

She had seen many changes over the last eighty years. The corporation tram that operated throughout the town which she caught at the top of Kingsthorpe had long since gone. The roads had been widened to accommodate three lanes and were now lined with supermarkets and drive-in fast-food outlets. Many of the houses once saw children playing in the street. Sadly, the children were now ensconced in their bedrooms talking to each other over social media. The only sound you'd hear in the street were the cars clipping kerbs as they reversed into tight spaces bumper to bumper.

Many of the original families had moved out a long time ago, and over the years the street had gradually turned into rental accommodation. There were a number of houses occupied by single people living in homes meant for multiple occupation, many of whom had either been homeless or fallen on hard times. No one talked to each other, but there was a tacit community spirit if one looked closer.

One day, Cole could smell something which Mika thought was sage wafting from the direction of Miss Hartwood's house. He also caught her posting letters in a rabbit hole next to a molehill. He asked her one day what she was doing.

"I asked them if they would please leave my garden and gave them directions to the common," she'd said in a very matter-of-fact way.

Cole chuckled as he told Mika. She looked out at his lawn and the rapidly disappearing vegetable patch, and then over at Miss Hartwood's thriving garden and her ginormous lettuces, cucumbers and bumper crop of carrots. Cole was out posting letters a few days later and didn't see a rabbit or pile of earth again.

Miss Hartwood was a deeply superstitious woman. She would not walk under ladders, cross people on the stairs and if she spilt salt, she threw it over her left shoulder, and she would never pick up the knives she dropped frequently. Mika would pick these up whenever she popped over to see if Miss Hartwood needed anything from the shops. One week, she counted seven knives, so goodness knows what Miss Hartwood used for cutting.

However, Miss Hartwood was very particular about one thing, and that was doors. She propped open all her internal doors with a brick or coping stone retrieved from skips and knitted them coverings in an assortment of colours. She insisted that all the doors were kept securely open because she had an absolute fear of slamming doors. She made sure that the windows were shut before any door was opened, and there were strategically placed wind chimes at the back and front door. Any visitor would be instructed on this custom, and woe betide anyone caught breaking the house rules.

On one particular occasion, Miss Hartwood was deep in conversation with Mika about the process of making pressed apple juice and without warning, she suddenly dashed off to the back door. A wind chime had announced that a door had broken from its moorings. Yes, Miss Hartwood was petrified of a slamming door.

When it came to healthcare, Miss Hartwood was invisible. She never visited a GP, and there was no record of who she was. She was never ill and didn't believe in the modern pill-popping culture. She grew herbs and had a small cottage garden outside her back door where she often brewed up medicinal concoctions for an array of illnesses.

When Mika had a bad chest infection and was confined to bed, Miss Hartwood prepared a tincture and left a bottle of a greenish liquid outside the back door. Cole followed the instructions Miss Hartwood meticulously wrote on the label and within days, Mika was out of bed with more energy than she'd ever had.

Miss Hartwood had a little orchard at the bottom of her garden and would often be seen climbing a rickety ladder picking the fruit. She placed the apples carefully in cardboard boxes making sure they didn't touch and would store them ready for Christmas. The windfalls would end up as jams and chutneys, and she would sell the rest of the crop.

Each year, she'd set up a trestle table under her bay window at the front of her house and display all her surplus soft fruit and vegetables along with the chutneys and jams. She had a sign beautifully painted in watercolours of trees and insects, listing the prices, and a large arrow to a small honesty box padlocked to the wall to leave money. It had a skull and crossbones on it to warn any thief of the consequences should they feel tempted. Strangely enough, no one ever did purloin anything despite the increasing burglaries in the area.

She made a steady income, which helped patch up some of the rotten window frames and to buy new plants or the odd piece of material so she could run up a new frock. Miss Hartwood was definitely a woman who belonged to the era of make do and mend.

Cole helped out when he could, but Miss Hartwood was a fiercely independent woman who loathed interference, often tutting and shaking her head if things weren't carried out precisely to her standard.

Many saw Miss Hartwood as an eccentric and a local curio, but they grew accustomed to seeing her walking along the busy high street with a parasol, wearing black glasses and dragging behind a trolley with a wonky wheel laden with items, many foraged on her travels. There was rhubarb from one house which had a sign declaring it to be free, and from a skip in the neighbouring street some wood, along with a bundle of flex she used to hang curtains. Cole and Mika grew fond of the elderly lady.

In her final years, Miss Hartwood pottered around her garden, Cole would run errands for her, and Mika would pop in each day as Miss Hartwood refused any help from strangers, especially if they were from the council, who she considered the devil incarnate. When Mika fussed, Miss Hartwood would scold her if she loitered too long and would often tell her to "run along home". But Mika worried about her falling, so she kept an eye on the back bedroom window where Miss Hartwood slept. Cole would check his watch, as at precisely nine-thirty each night the lamp was turned off and Mika, feeling a sense of relief, could sleep easily. It was a ritual practised each night.

When Cole's mother was taken ill, the hospital warned to expect the worst and encouraged him to agree for her not to be resuscitated. Miss Hartwood waved her hand that she'd never heard such poppycock and handed Mika a list of items she needed to make a posset. Mika gathered the ingredients from the garden and a small independent health shop, which Miss Hartwood approved of, and handed them over to her. Miss Hartwood chopped, steamed and sieved a liquid until set into a small heatproof bowl and handed it to Mika with strict instructions on how the mixture had to be taken. Mika held the posset carefully as she walked over to Cole's car. She could feel Miss Hartwood's eyes burning into the back of her head as she stood watching. She nodded in approval while waving them off.

Cole smuggled the container under his jacket when entering the ward. The nurses were huddled around the nurses' station deep in conversation. He paused when Mika placed a box of chocolates on the desk. The nurses shifted their attention and swooped like carrion crows pouncing on their prey as they devoured the chocolates. It gave Cole precious time to head to his mother's bed undetected.

Mika darted around the bed pulling the curtains before Cole placed the posset on the side table. His mother looked so frail and restless; her eyes flickered and then closed again. Cole looked over at his wife, who nodded. He lifted the posset as Mika gently raised Cole's mother's head. Just for a brief moment, she looked at her son when he placed the edge of the container next to her lips. Her mouth yielded once the substance entered her body. She coughed, and Cole wiped her mouth. Mika gently returned her head to the lumpy pillow. She then went to the foot of the bed and checked the hospital chart and Miss

Hartwood's written instructions. She wouldn't have any food until eight the next morning which gave the posset time to act. Mika swiftly pulled back the curtains while Cole sat down talking to his mother.

During the night, Cole's mother tossed and turned with perspiration covering her body. The doctor was called. He stood looking at the frail creature and shook his head. Knowing she was nearing death, he instructed a nurse to wipe the elderly woman's forehead and advised to have the trolley ready to take her down to Rose Cottage, the mortuary. The ward manager rang Cole and urged him to come quickly due to his mother's deterioration.

Mika and Cole rushed down the long, empty corridor, the only sound being the echo of their shoes and the gentle buzzing of the flickering strip lighting as they approached the nurses' station where a nurse sat texting. Mika leant over, causing the young woman to jolt backwards and promptly push her phone under a stack of files.

She stood up and escorted them over to Cole's mother's bed. Mika asked for a cup of tea, but the nurse shrugged saying that they'd have to wait until morning. So, Mika and Cole sat either side of the bed, each taking turns to wipe the perspiration from her head and arms, and they waited. Cole dozed off as Mika continued to wring out the sodden flannel into a small bowl. Exhausted, Mika sat back in her chair and felt a hand on her shoulder along with the smell of lavender. It was such a reassuring feeling. She looked around expecting to see one of the relatives offering support, but no one was there.

The rattling of the tea trolley stirred Cole. He yawned and stretched, and then looked over at his wife sitting huddled up in the chair with her coat pulled tightly around her. She looked so restful. And his mother; she was fast asleep and her breathing steadier.

A woman handed him a cup of tea and a biscuit. He asked for another and placed one next to Mika. As he sat back down, he heard a voice requesting a strong cup of tea with plenty of sugar. He looked over to his mother, who was now sitting up in bed combing her hair. Mika awoke and clasped her hands when she looked at his mother and then at Cole, who winked. The fuss attracted the ward manager who was walking past. She sighed heavily updating the patient's chart and instructed the trolley to go to Ward 6. There would be no departures to Rose Cottage today. Cole's mother made a complete recovery and was discharged three days later.

Cole and Mika travelled back home a few days later. They'd been away longer than anticipated and were greeted with a mountain of letters. Mika wanted to go round to see Miss Hartwood, but felt exhausted and complained of a head cold and then began sneezing. Cole instructed her to go to bed straight away saying that he'd bring her a hot toddy. They could both go across to Miss Hartwood tomorrow to thank her and give her some of the plums he'd picked from his mother's garden. Mika did as her husband instructed, and Cole poured himself a small whiskey, which was his usual pick-me-up. He also poured his wife a brandy to which he added some hot water. He left it on the side before winding up the clock on the mantelpiece, and then he sat down to rest his eyes.

It was the clock striking one which stirred him. It was pitch dark, and he stumbled towards the light switch before climbing the stairs. He was so tired that he slipped under the duvet and snuggled next to Mika. They both drifted off so deeply that neither of them heard the slamming door in the distance.

Mika was up later than normal the next morning while Cole lay fast asleep. She pulled out the clothes from the washing machine. They had a musty smell, so she threw them back in, added more washing powder and set the machine for a long cycle. She headed out to the back garden to replenish the bird table, and then she thought she'd go over to see Miss Hartwood with the plums, help with any errands and flick a duster around after she'd finished placing a few nuts in a hollow of the beech tree. A squirrel often trapezed into the garden as magpies divebombed it away from their territory, but it always managed to outsmart them with its agility.

It was waiting, and Mika smiled as the animal approached her. She held out her hand, and the squirrel snatched the nuts and darted up the tree. She flung back her head in laughter and it was then that she noticed Miss Hartwood's bedroom curtains – they were still drawn and her lamp was still on.

There was an inquest as Miss Hartwood had had no contact with any medical professional during the last thirty years. The coroner couldn't believe a woman in her late eighties didn't have any history at the GP surgery, which had many doctors over the years, or at the local hospital, and that her records were typed up on foolscap paper and found in a box in an old filing cabinet. Her death was recorded as natural causes.

As she had no relatives, Mika and Cole arranged the funeral and a small gathering afterwards at the local village hall, where Miss Hartwood had displayed fruits, flowers and vegetables from her garden in previous years and would often leave with rosettes and cups.

The local newspaper sent a reporter because Miss Hartwood had contributed to a health page previously and was interviewed on local radio. Unbeknown to many, she had a following, and people turned up to see her. A lady dressed head to foot in canary yellow talked to Mika about how Miss Hartwood cured her arthritis. A young woman told Cole how Miss Hartwood had helped with her son's temper tantrums when everyone else had written him off as too complex. Two homeless people paid their respects and told Mika that Miss Hartwood would often bring them sandwiches and pots of chutney. Mika chatted about going to see Cole's mother and how Miss Hartwood had talked about seeing a figure standing in her bedroom doorway each night. It was strange. Miss Hartwood was not senile and appeared very lucid and could recite the balcony scene from *Romeo and Juliet* word perfect.

Mika was sure from the description Miss Hartwood had given that the figure was her sister. She remembered her talking about Felicity. She was the adventurous one, wanting to go to sea and often spending her time playing near the canal. One day, she was stretching across near the weir to pick some juicy blackberries, when she lost her footing and plunged into the water. A rip current dragged her under. The official cause of death was drowning. Miss Hartwood knew otherwise. She told Mika that Felicity's fate had been sealed a few days before when in a fit of temper, she had slammed the parlour door. Her father was furious and gave chase. Miss Hartwood remembered her mother rushing from room to room chanting something and sprinkling lavender and salt. It was after this tragic event that Miss Hartwood's family made sure all the doors were always firmly secure.

Sadly, Miss Hartwood's home was put up for sale. Mika and Cole seriously thought about putting in an offer as they felt it wrong a stranger moving in. Mika suggested that perhaps if they bought the house, they could set it up as a working museum or a home for retired naturopaths, if such a home was needed. But it was too late: the house was sold even before the "For Sale" sign had gone up. There was a list of people interested in moving into the street as it was one of the few areas still affordable. Mika struggled to sleep worrying about who was going to move in. Cole told her not to be so silly as no modern family would want a house like Miss Hartwood's because there was far too much work to be undertaken. The whole place would need rewiring, a new roof and goodness knows what else to bring it up to the standard demanded of a family today.

Mr and Mrs Boyd were a modern family who moved into Miss Hartwood's. They knocked down the internal walls and pulled out the original features and changed it to a huge open-plan space. The windows were replaced with UPVC triple glazing. The low community brick walls at the back had huge wooden panels pushed against them creating shadows, which stunted the growth of Cole's raspberries. The fruit trees were cut down and a large orange trampoline complete with fairy lights landed. Decking was placed over Miss Hartwood's mature herb garden that she had tended over the years, and it was now a space created for the weekly BBQ.

Cole went out each morning before eight o'clock to do some weeding or mow the lawn. He enjoyed pottering around the garden, and he would have the radio on low which he'd hum to. Mr Boyd would venture out sometime after eight-thirty and stand outside coughing as he lit up a cigarette. He had raised the patio area which allowed him to see into Cole and Mika's back garden. He would talk to Cole as he knelt weeding amongst the rose beds and complain about his bad back, the buzzing in his ears and his throbbing haemorrhoids. Each day, if Cole didn't time it right, he'd get a daily commentary on Mr Boyd's medical conditions, none of which prevented him from walking down to the shed, lugging a large petrol mower up the path, which he laid weeks earlier, and pushing it around the narrow lawn, bashing into the bushes. He'd then trim the hedges, scoop up the cuttings and place them into bags as the children darted around screaming and throwing balls at each other on the trampoline, which more often than not would bounce over into Cole's flower beds, decapitating his prized dahlias.

Cole and Mika decided to retire as they were both now sixty-five years old. It was something they'd planned for the last few years. In preparation, they had bought a small cottage in Derbyshire which they visited most weekends.

One morning, Cole was walking back from the newsagents with a newspaper and a magazine for Mika when he saw a sign strapped to a lamp post announcing that a planning application had been submitted for Miss Hartwood's house to have a loft conversion and a balcony at the back. Cole was furious and hurried home to write a letter of objection. Despite his best efforts, including support from a local councillor, the planning permission was granted.

Weeks later, trucks arrived and machinery was unloaded. At precisely nine o'clock each morning drilling, hammering and loud voices commenced, which continued throughout the day until nine at night. Cole and Mika would then have to contend with raised voices and the children running around. Cole thought about contacting the Environmental Health department, but Mika urged him not to, so the weekends away to Derbyshire increased and they extended their visits to a week here and there. Gradually, they moved more of their belongings with the intention of setting up permanent residence there. Cole suggested that perhaps it was time for them to move on. Mika nodded sadly as they drove away to spend a fortnight in Derbyshire.

Each time Mika and Cole returned home, something else had been added to Miss Hartwood's house. A grey resin door with bright white lights had replaced the ornate stained-glass door with a William Morris motif. Miss Hartwood's house was now overrun with laminate flooring, which intensified the sound of the children running around. Gone was the tasteful decoration in keeping with the house, and now dull, grey walls appeared with a huge TV screen fastened to one side. There was scaffolding on the front to put up solar panels; the trellis which had supported the wisteria Miss Hartwood's father had planted was ripped down and thrown into a skip to make way for grey shutters. Mrs Boyd liked the old rustic look and stood admiring the louvre panels and how they improved the house.

Mika and Cole would relax in the evenings watching their favourite TV shows. Sadly, this was often interrupted by the sounds of Mrs Boyd's shrieking cries as she screamed at her husband. Mr Boyd would boom back in their arguments over money, the children, the state of the house and the fact that he didn't work. Cole's knuckles turned white as he gripped the side of the chair. Mika turned up the volume of the television to drown out the wailing. She tried reasoning with her husband that bringing up a family wasn't easy and they'd settle down over the coming weeks, but the tensions next door grew.

One of the daughters would shout from the top of the new loft conversion down to her mother. Mika knew everything that happened in Miss Hartwood's house as she could hear conversations about their daughter's grades, her friends, and Mrs Boyd's new job as a community liaison officer. Mrs Boyd would shriek when her husband cooked because he'd set off the smoke alarm, the sound intensifying as he flung open the back door. And then came the slamming doors.

The girls slammed the front door when they left to go out with friends. Mrs Boyd slammed the kitchen door when Mr Boyd was sitting in the back garden, smoking. Cole couldn't stand it anymore and instructed Mika to pack. They were going up to Derbyshire with a view to touring the Peak District.

Cole and Mika returned after three weeks away exhausted after a long drive back but stress-free. The country air had relaxed them both. Cole went straight to bed and fell fast asleep, appearing nonplussed as he put in his earplugs. Mika relaxed in a bath of

Epsom salts – a remedy Miss Hartwood had passed on to her. She read afterwards until dozing off.

It must have been two in the morning when Mika stirred. At first, she thought Cole had said something, but he was fast asleep. She turned over and pulled up the duvet, but the noises grew louder. She sat up and listened. It was a child giggling, and it was coming from the direction of Miss Hartwood's house. Mika thought that perhaps the girls were having a sleepover. Mika moved her head closer to the wall. The voices grew louder, but they weren't the Boyd girls. Mika then listened to a woman's raised voice. Perhaps it was Mrs Boyd talking to a guest. No, the voice was more clipped with received pronunciation. Mika's eyes widened as she listened. She recognised the voice. It was Miss Hartwood.

Mika didn't want to mention anything about the voice to Cole. He appeared relaxed after their time away and he'd arranged another getaway in a few weeks' time which he was looking forward to. She watched him singing as he cleaned the car, and then a van arrived at Miss Hartwood's. Bags of cement were unloaded and positioned on the pavement. A woman tried to edge past with a pram; Mr Boyd suggested she ought to go on the road. Cole witnessed an argument between Mr Boyd and the young mother and how he stood blocking her path. She pointed to the pram and her child crying, but Mr Boyd stood in her way. She backed up and continued on the road. Mr Boyd then, with the help of another man, began shovelling cement into the churning cement mixer in readiness for the new front wall, creating a mess all over the pavement. Cole took a deep breath and went back into his house. Mika stood by the window.

She reassured him that it was only temporary and given it was outside, the sound wouldn't disturb them.

That evening, Mr and Mrs Boyd's children screamed and ran around the house, Mrs Boyd shrieked, and Mr Boyd bellowed. Cole snapped that he'd call the Environmental Health department first thing in the morning. He looked at the clock and frantically wrote things down on a writing pad from the bedside cabinet.

A week later, a tall, gangly man appeared at Cole and Mika's door holding a black case. He held up his identity card, and Mika showed him into the lounge. They both listened as he explained the process and supplied listening devices that had to be set against the walls. These would trigger and record loud sounds. He also gave them incident diaries to complete each time they heard a noise as it was important to gather evidence. Mika didn't like the idea of snooping on anyone and just thought the family was going through a rough time. The Environmental Health officer encouraged them to record sounds which impacted them because it was important to gather information for a noise abatement order. Cole nodded in agreement, and the man placed the devices against the adjoining walls to Miss Hartwood's house.

Over the next few days, noises from Miss Hartwood's were unusually quiet. Mika thought that perhaps Environmental Health had informed the Boyds. Cole agreed, but took no chances and still stuck his bright orange earplugs into each ear. They made Mika laugh as they looked like carrots sticking out from the side of his head.

Mika slept well for a few nights but was awoken one night by the sound of giggling. She pulled herself up half asleep and then heard a familiar voice. It was Miss Hartwood's again, followed by the sounds of footsteps. She looked at Cole and wondered whether she should wake him. He was lying on his side, fast asleep. She settled down once again and began to drift off only to be woken by the sound of a slamming door and also Miss Hartwood's voice. She shook her head. Surely she must be hallucinating. She'd call her GP and make an appointment. It was probably nothing, and a sympathetic doctor would give her something to sleep. She wouldn't tell Cole – he'd only worry.

The next day, the Boyds had a blazing row. Mrs Boyd returned from work early and promptly launched into a tirade over the state of the house. Mr Boyd tried to appease, but her shrieking voice caused Cole to rush to the incident diaries and frantically scribble everything down. He encouraged Mika to do the same, but she feigned some excuse as she busied herself going to hang out the washing, and she was preoccupied with the consequences of involving Environmental Health. She really didn't like all this fuss, but there were the voices. It couldn't be Miss Hartwood's voice she'd heard for the past couple of nights. And then something strange happened.

She was hanging out the last of the washing, and standing on the footstool to raise up the line, when she caught Mr Boyd standing by the back door. He was standing completely motionless. Mika didn't see him sway or anything. He looked like a statue. At first she thought he was looking at something, so she followed his line of sight, but there was nothing there. A magpie swooped down, but Mr Boyd didn't flinch. He simply stood staring.

Mika went back inside and prepared dinner. It was over the rhubarb crumble that Cole disclosed what he'd seen earlier. He'd returned from the tip when he saw Mrs Boyd with her two daughters walking up the road not saying a single word and just staring straight ahead. He watched them cross the road without looking, causing a motorist to swerve, but they continued staring straight ahead as though following someone. Even stranger was that they were heading in the direction of the canal.

The Environmental Health officer called round to collect the devices and incident diaries, and announced he'd write to them within ten days with the results. His response was encouraging; Cole put his arm around his wife. But Mika protested, worried that they were a young family with a lot going on. She thought they'd been much quieter lately. Cole shrugged and reassured her it was the right thing to do; if it was a statutory nuisance, the law dictates there are consequences.

He lectured her about the law being there for a reason, and that without it, society would break down. Mika thought it pointless to argue as Cole was on his high horse. She made an excuse and went upstairs to have a lie down. She was exhausted. Cole felt guilty and made her some scrambled eggs and a cup of tea and took them up to her. He placed a photograph on the tray he'd found while sorting through some letters in his bureau. It was a picture of Miss Hartwood standing proudly in her orchard next to a bumper crop of apples, pears and plums. She grew the old varieties, and the local newspaper ran a story about Miss Hartwood, with her quoting that the last time there had been such a crop was on VE day. Mika smiled thinking of the times she'd helped Miss Hartwood gather her harvest and how precise she'd been in distributing the apples into labelled boxes. She looked away and wiped her eyes. How she wished Miss Hartwood still lived next door.

The next day, Cole was out mowing the lawn. He'd set up the table with breakfast cereal, a bowl of stewed fruits and an assortment of preserves. He left Mika still fast asleep in bed; he knew she was still upset with all the business about the Environmental Health officer. She stirred just a little after eight-thirty, after a good night's sleep – Cole had suggested she take one of Miss Hartwood's herbal remedies of lavender and valerian, which worked a treat.

She took a leisurely stroll downstairs and picked up a couple of letters from the doormat. One was official looking, which she assumed was from Environmental Health. She placed them against the clock on the mantelpiece. They could wait until later, and she continued out onto the patio to join Cole.

The sun was streaming down, and the usual squirrel was sitting on the fence waiting. Mika took a handful of nuts and went over. The squirrel ran towards her and before she opened her hands, it brushed its face against her body. She then looked up at a wood pigeon nestling on the top of Miss Hartwood's chimney, cooing. She'd not witnessed that for some time. Also, Cole commented while pouring his wife a cup of tea that he hadn't seen Mr Boyd outside smoking.

The days passed and still there was no sight of the Boyds. Cole suggested that perhaps they'd gone away abroad or were staying with relatives. Mika agreed as they could have gone on holiday, but she changed her mind when pottering upstairs and looking into Miss Hartwood's back garden, where she saw a stack of folded-up washing on one of the chairs. She also noticed that the back window was open, to which Cole suggested that perhaps they'd just been in a hurry. But there was something niggling Mika because Mr Boyd would never leave a downstairs window open. He was obsessed about security. Mika suggested calling round just to make sure. Cole reluctantly agreed; otherwise, he knew his wife would carry on talking about it.

He knocked on the Boyds' front door. There was no answer. He looked through the window but didn't see anything out of the ordinary. There were newspapers on the coffee table and a jacket flung on the back of the settee. He lifted the latch on the back gate and entered the back garden. He saw the washing on the chair and felt it. It was damp with insects crawling around. Mrs Boyd must have forgotten, although he thought it strange as they were usually out in the garden during the evening. Then, as he was leaving, he saw a parcel pushed against one of the dustbins. Cole bent down and looked at it, seeing that the Royal Mail date stamp was more than a fortnight ago. Still, they may have forgotten if they'd got a last-minute deal to go abroad, as Cole suggested while they sat discussing the matter over dinner later.

The Boyds hadn't been seen now for over four weeks, so Mika urged Cole to contact the police. The police were reluctant at first, but they decided to act when the school reported that the two girls hadn't been seen for weeks despite their teachers calling to check on them. They searched the house and went to visit Mrs Boyd's employer. They hadn't seen her either, and she hadn't booked time off for annual leave. They did mention that there had been problems a few weeks previously after she came into work upset. No, they didn't think she was at risk from personal harm and weren't aware of any domestic issues, but there was something about her behaviour. She wasn't herself. Relatives were contacted, but no one knew their whereabouts.

After eight weeks, there was a press appeal and the police issued a statement of concern. The house became a local attraction, and people would stop, point and talk about the mysterious disappearance of the Boyds.

A local paranormal group wanted to hold a night vigil, causing rumours to spread that Miss Hartwood's house was somehow connected with the Boyds disappearing. Although, what was certain were the strange events that occurred around the time of their disappearance.

The Environmental Health officer's report found that the family had created a statutory noise nuisance. He played a sample of the sound. Cole frowned and looked at his wife. She listened carefully. It was not any of the Boyds' voices they heard. They both looked at each other and nodded.

It was Miss Hartwood.

The Boyds were never found, and the house went back on the market, but each time it sold the sale fell through. There were also reports of singing coming from the garden and a light seen from the back bedroom, which would disappear at precisely nine-thirty every night.

DNA

Avril Phipps looked at the financial statement and moved her finger down line by line looking at the total sum displayed at the bottom of the page. £350,000 was the amount she had been awarded. This represented twenty years of marriage, a sixteen-year-old daughter, and a house that had been sold with the equity split on a sixty-forty basis in her favour. Her ex-husband, Daniel, moved out twelve months ago and had set up home with an ingénue.

Avril walked around the lounge which was once crammed with oriental rugs, antiques and objects of virtue, but now stood barren. As she opened the patio door an autumnal breeze seeped through, her thoughts turning to the garden and down the Cotswold stone pathway to the sunken patio and the laurel bushes she'd planted. Originally, she had wanted box hedging.

"Takes too long to mature. I'd go for cherry laurel," she was advised. They were now dense and over thirty feet high. Also the hydrangeas she'd tended over the years. "Not the right soil, love," Daniel had claimed. Undeterred, Avril brought in acid-rich soil. They'd bloomed, and this year they were at their best. And the rowan tree with its orange berries, a gift from her grandmother, greeted her as she approached the orchard. "Let's do something with the garden," Daniel had said, waving down from a tree. He always did odd things that made her laugh. And so, they both cultivated the grassy knoll.

Daniel hired a cultivator, and Avril strimmed around the edges. They planted a different variety of trees. A quince tree once sat majestically at the bottom of the orchard. "When the quince dies, there'd be a death in the family," she recalled her grandmother saying when she was young. The quince began to struggle and no matter what Avril did, it didn't recover.

"An old wives' tale," Daniel had said. But a few months after their marriage, it withered and eventually died.

Work took Daniel away from home for longer, and then they had separate bedrooms, and then his disclosure quite casually over an evening meal of salmon en croute: "I've met someone else. I'm sorry. I didn't mean this to happen. I'll go upstairs and pack after dessert." That was Daniel – he always had a sweet tooth.

He had met Angelica at the gym, and he went on to give a rough outline of their meeting and her description. "She needs someone to take her in hand." Daniel was generous with his time.

"I never liked him anyway. Always smiling and laughing. And at his age too!" her mother, Clarissa had hissed. "He was the cunning type. Pretends not to be interested, but plots. Yes, a cunning type chasing some tart. Retribution will serve its hand." She held many superstitions.

Her mother popped over to help Avril pack and sat on a plastic patio chair in the lounge looking around the room. "I've never liked this house. It's big and boxy, no character. It needs flattening if you ask me. Get something ultramodern and go and live life to the full." Clarissa didn't like anything older than herself. "Gives you a chance to declutter and get rid of all those relics." She waved her hand towards the figurines sitting on the side ready to be packed.

Avril had found a new house. She wanted a new start and closed her eyes and put a pin in a map. She vowed that wherever it landed she'd move to. Although, she did have a number of conditions: it couldn't be further north than Northampton and not too far east. It landed in East Anglia.

While it was more easterly than Cambridgeshire, the area was attractive. The house was smaller but more historical and, importantly, she got more for her money, so she could bag a bit of history into the bargain.

Avril floated the brochure onto her mother's lap. "My new house."

Clarissa leafed through the pages. "Aren't there any new-builds? The ceilings are too low and just think how many people have died in there." She pulled a face of disgust as she looked at a picture of the bedroom with eaves and beams over the bed. "Probably hung themselves."

Equally, Casey wasn't impressed. "Selfish cow!" She stormed upstairs. "You never think about me!" she screamed before slamming her bedroom door.

Looking at a chip in her cup, her mother said, "She'll come round in time."

Avril had sketched out designs and collected a number of material samples. She wanted an arts and crafts style with a twist of New England. "Different blues or perhaps a little grey to contrast. I'll have the same colour scheme throughout downstairs, and go to mocha and neutral tones upstairs," she soliloquised. Avril liked interior design and thought about running her own business. "There are lots of cottage industries around, and I was thinking of dropping a day at work and perhaps going part-time."

"But why East Anglia, Avril? It's shoved up there in the corner." Her mother pointed her finger in mid-air. "And it's hardly convenient," she added, watching Avril take things out of a sideboard drawer and place them into boxes.

She had been sifting through items and putting what was hers in one pile and the others for Daniel or the charity shop. "It's odd really; I always liked the place. Daniel and I stayed there quite a few times when we got married... His ancestors came from there." She looked at her mother, who was nodding while leafing through the brochure. "Strange, as I remember Dad going on about his grandmother coming from there."

Clarissa ignored the reference to her ex-husband and continued to look through the brochure. "Really," she uttered. "Fancy, and I thought they came from Milton Keynes. All I seem to remember is going round a lot of roundabouts." Her mother looked up and rolled her eyes.

"I've had a yearning for the place," replied Avril, taking no notice of her comments.

Clarissa put down the brochure. "Avril, there's something else. I can tell you're being far too gushy and matter-of-fact." She then locked eyes on what Avril was holding.

"Adrian gave me this."

One of her mother's eyebrows arched as she mouthed, "Adrian."

"He works at the estate agents. It's a welcome present. They bought a job lot I suppose to drum up trade."

Her mother was still hovering over the word "Adrian".

"It's so simple and…" Avril held up a slim white box.

"What is it?" Clarissa sat up.

Avril walked over and handed it to her. "It's a DNA test."

"Pandora's box," her mother scoffed. "DNA, it's all a load of rubbish. I don't understand why you would do such a thing." She pushed the box back, sipped her coffee and winced. "I will get you an expresso machine."

Avril sat down. "I wasn't going to bother, but Adrian…"

Her mother looked at her and mouthed "Adrian" again and nodded.

"He said all I had to do was provide a saliva sample."

Still flicking through the brochure, Clarissa was only half listening. "They do have some new-builds." She then peered over the top of the booklet. "Adrian must be on a commission. I thought he was selling houses, not shares in the Human Genome Project."

"It's fascinating." Avril opened the box and took out an envelope. "You can connect with relatives via this site, and it's just amazing to see who you're related to."

Shaking her head, her mother said, "A box of no-good. DNA – the only good use for that is to catch serial killers and philandering husbands. I suppose this Adrian will be coming round to do your plumbing next!"

Avril ignored her mother's barbed comments. "I've already been doing some research." She opened the envelope.

"It will all end in tears. You mark my words." Clarissa flung the brochure onto the coffee table. "I'd better be going." As she got up, her cup slipped and fell to the floor. The handle broke off. "You see – a bad omen." She bent down and scooped up the remnants.

Casey stomped around upstairs banging drawers and dragging something along the floor.

"But you haven't let me finish. I found that originally…" Avril followed her mother into the kitchen as she tossed the cup into the bin. "I could've glued the handle back on." Avril stood holding her research as her mother put on rubber gloves and started doing the washing up. "Twenty percent of me is Spanish with a mixture of French, Italian and a smattering of the Baltics, with the majority English and from the East Anglian region. Can you believe that?" Avril laughed.

Clarissa clanked around the sink. "For those who like that sort of thing, that is the sort of thing they like."

Avril looked at her puzzled. "I thought you'd be happy." Her mother continued washing up.

"I'm going."

"What else do I have?" She looked out across the garden. "I have no marriage and a stroppy teenager who is so bloody totally self-absorbed!" Avril shouted towards the ceiling.

A loud stomping sound responded.

Clarissa took off the rubber gloves and wiped down the surfaces. "It's not natural. These DNA tests and all these genealogy whatsits – it stirs up trouble, and it's all in the past." She waved the cloth as she talked.

Avril knew her mother loathed the past. Her father had walked out on them when Avril was ten years old. Her stepdad then came on the scene until Clarissa walked out on him, taking Avril with her.

"Probably too many home truths I suspect, Mother." Her mother turned and flicked the wet cloth in her face.

"All I can say is let sleeping dogs lie. It's from your father's side, so it will be just trouble. I can sense trouble and I can see storm clouds above, so just leave it and go and live in Spain. There are some lovely properties in Almeria, or at least buy a new-build and secure your future rather than picking up someone else's woes." Clarissa gave her a peck on the cheek, and then sniffed. "And you're still wearing white musk." She walked into the hall to collect her coat and bag. "I'm off, Casey! Do try and be nice, dear, to your mum – she is going through a lot!" she shouted up the stairs. "Even if she needs to be housed in a maximum secure mental hospital," she whispered while leaving the house.

Casey gave her mother the cold shoulder from the time they left Bedfordshire until nearly three weeks after moving into the thatched circa seventeenth-century cottage in East Anglia. She only broke the silence out of necessity when she couldn't get an internet connection.

"How am I supposed to survive like this?" she screamed at Avril. Her mother stood with a glass of wine and gesticulated towards the ceiling.

"Try moving closer to the window. I'm sure you'll get a passing Wi-Fi connection." Casey stomped off, slamming the lounge door, and stormed upstairs. "Or perhaps if we get one of those booster things!" Avril shouted after her daughter. Casey jumped up and down on the floor above. "I wouldn't do that, Casey. I don't think these ceilings can take your weight." Avril took another sip of her wine and laughed. She could hear Casey on the phone bitching about her.

Avril relaxed, poured another drink and walked out into the garden. It wasn't as large as the last one, but it was mature and had a nice natural screen of shrubs. She could hear voices and laughing as she walked around the garden, taking more sips of her wine. Slipping off her shoes, she listened to the wood pigeons nestling in the white willow tree. And then the laughter died away and she could hear humming. Avril perched herself on the side of one of the wooden raised beds. The humming became louder. She thought it was choir practice, but as she listened it was chanting. She swayed slightly and took another sip of her wine. The chanting filled the garden and her eyes felt heavy. It was such an effort to keep them open as they flickered and then closed as the chanting surrounded her. She drifted off deeper and her wine glass slipped from her hand. She awoke. As she rubbed her eyes, she could see dark figures in the distance.

The welcoming committee stood on the doorstep. "I'm Corenza and this is Prudence."

A tall woman with prominent teeth leant forward. "Please, call me Pru."

"And I'm Verity," said a smaller woman, peeping round.

Corenza held out a basket. "Welcome to Clamount Stroud. We bring you good tidings. My darling nephew Adrian." She flashed a smile at Avril. "Of Partlington Estate Agency." Avril nodded. "He's simply in raptures about you. You've become a bit of celeb."

Avril felt she had little choice but to invite them in.

The women squeezed over the threshold and buzzed around going from one room to another. "I do love your colour scheme."

Pru brushed her hand along the top of the sofa. "Oh, that's nice."

Corenza held up one of Avril's figurines and looked at the base. She nodded over to Verity. "Very nice."

Avril tried to direct them into the kitchen with a view of ushering them onto the patio, but it was like herding cats.

Verity hovered around the cloakroom as Pru was fascinated with the Chinese lacquer cabinet, and Corenza with her Ormolu clock. "You have such good taste."

Eventually, with the smell of coffee and the sight of a Victoria sponge, they fluttered outside.

"You must join our committee." Corenza went into detail about their good deeds. "We're simply brimming with ideas." She continued without drawing breath about the money they raised for the church. "Such an amazing Norman Saxon example." She beamed. "The village hall is another fine example of wonderful architecture. I wouldn't at all be surprised if Charles II was ensconced there."

"And the paperchases – they go down well with the cadets," Verity said in a breathy voice. "I just love running ahead and planning the routes, and all those boys trying to catch up like bloodhounds."

Avril looked at Verity's generous bosoms and imagined her enjoying being ravished. "And such good exercise to get your steps in," she gushed.

"Absolutely," Corenza crowed, her blue eyes framed with lashings of black mascara.

Corenza nodded towards Verity and Pru. "That's settled. You're now part of the committee. We'll have so much fun."

"Why, that's too kind," replied Avril, holding up her cup. She smiled hard until her face ached.

"Mr Ouspensky will like you so much." Corenza looked at Avril, who could only think of why the hell she'd been talked around by the three old bags.

Casey had joined a sixth-form college in the neighbouring town of St Tinden-Regis. "I'll pick you up at five." Casey looked at Avril and grunted a response before sloping off towards a glass building. Avril wanted her to be happy. She wasn't an easy child.

"Difficult that one. She'll be just like her father," Avril's mother had declared. "She's trouble – too self-centred. I blame you, Avril. You're too available for her."

As she watched her daughter stop on the steps and chat to a group of youngsters, Avril went through the day's list in her head. She had a couple of meetings over the internet and on the phone, and then she'd bake a cake for the committee meeting tonight about raising funds for the new excavation of a historic site near the church. Avril watched Casey laughing. "The move will take time" – that's what she'd told her. It was the right thing moving away; it gave her time to mourn and recover from the marriage. She didn't want Casey hurt, but it was Avril who was hurting.

The investment she'd put into the marriage, and then Angelica coming along and swooping up Daniel. Avril was still furious about the divided loyalty of their mutual friends, many of whom had evaporated into thin air. Her telephone calls went straight to voicemail and texts didn't get a response. She felt abandoned and wounded. And Angelica flaunting her youth. Avril looked at herself in the car mirror.

"You must wear a higher sun factor," she could hear her mother saying. "You don't want to add to those crow's feet." Clarissa was good at pointing things out.

Casey disappeared into the building with the group chatting and laughing. "She'll soon fit in. Kids are malleable," Avril told herself as she drove off, still going through her mental list and what cake she would bake.

Later at the committee meeting, a tall man stood by a stack of chairs. "A new recruit." The man's large paws clasped Avril's hands.

"Mr Ouspensky?"

He nodded. "Please, Aaron, and welcome, my dear. I've heard so much about you, and so high up in PR. We are honoured for such an illustrious person to join our humble committee. And your name begins with an 'A', too." He continued to stare at Avril, smiling. He had large brown eyes that appeared not to blink. Avril felt her hands aching as she attempted to remove herself from his grip, but it intensified.

Corenza, Pru and Verity then appeared from nowhere.

"There you are. You're so good." Corenza looked at Avril's cake. "Simply delish. We'll raffle it tonight, and it will push a few more coffers into the old pot."

Mr Ouspensky beamed and finally let go of her hands. "Such wonderful things are happening. I see we'll have a good year – a bumper crop, so to speak." Corenza, Pru and Verity laughed.

Avril watched him talking to the women and each one of them nodding. He then paused and looked around at Avril. Avril felt awkward and broke his gaze. She turned and walked towards a group of women fussing over a map.

"We will start here, and fireworks here too." An older woman dressed in tweed stood pointing.

Avril continued to walk around the room. A group of men huddled in the corner played dominoes. A tall, spindly lady filled up the tea urn. "Another cup, dear?" Avril refused and sat down.

Mr Ouspensky was still deep in discussion with Corenza, Pru and Verity. Perhaps her mother was right about buying a new-build. People on new developments were too busy living an insular, minimalist lifestyle to bother you.

Corenza snorted as she laughed and looked around at Avril and waved. Avril returned the gesture and looked up at the tall baroque-style ceiling. Her gaze followed the beams resting on plaster busts. The busts were of men and women in mediaeval costume. She looked away, but something caught her attention. Just for a moment, she felt their eyes looking down on her.

Later that night, Casey was going out to meet two friends, Amber and Chase, who both lived in the village. Avril stood at the gate. "You will write, won't you?" she called. Casey looked round, and then put up her hood.

Avril laughed as she straightened the recycling boxes and pushed down one of the lids. The wine bottles rattled under the force. "Too much drinking results in broken capillaries," her mother's voice reminded her as she pushed down harder on the lid until it was fully closed.

She looked up at the trees. They were all spindly dark shadows that looked skeletal against the wintery sky. The garden had drifted off into a winter's sleep. A shooting star shot across the night sky. "Make a wish, make a wish." She clasped her hands and closed her eyes tightly. "A simple life, like the old days, just going back to the old ways," she whispered. She continued to walk around the patio and stood lost in thought. She'd been in Clamount Stroud for over four months now. She had made the right decision as she stood looking upwards. Things weren't that bad. She remembered snatches of a conversation a few weeks after moving in.

"Our big event is on St Mark's Eve," Corenza had declared, her eyes bigger than any dinner plate.

"We follow all the old traditions here in Clamount Stroud," said Verity, giggling.

"We're all direct descendants," Pru said with a snort.

It was the last comment which had made Avril remember the results of her DNA test. "Me too. I'm connected to the area – more neighbouring villages I suppose." She remembered Adrian asking about the results.

"We keep a spreadsheet. It's about local history. You wouldn't mind?"

Avril had thought it was a nice idea and had volunteered her lineage. She'd also been doing some of her own research. "I'm a direct descendant of a Hawksworth, although I'm having trouble finding out much about them."

"Incomplete records – such a nuisance. I had the same trouble, too," said Corenza. Pru and Verity nodded.

"All a long time ago, and we're probably all part of something or other." Avril had laughed. She remembered the three of them looking at her. Their faces were blank.

"You'll just love St Mark's Eve." Corenza clasped her hands. The three of them looked at each other. "Dressing up and the village, it just comes alive." Avril remembered Corena flailing her arms around, laughing.

It was now getting cold, so Avril headed towards the back door, but she could hear voices. At first she thought it was singing, but as she listened the voices became clearer. It was chanting. She felt a sense of unease as she slipped back inside and bolted the back door.

The next day, Casey stood on the doorstep and pecked her grandmother on the cheek. "Hello, Gran."

"You've changed your tune. The East Anglian air must be paying dividends. Are you dating?" Casey blushed.

Avril was standing behind Clarissa. "Quick sticks, Mother, I'm getting cold." Avril gave her mother a gentle shove to get into the warmth of the hallway.

"Manners! I'm only staying three days, so no pleading. I won't stay a day longer. The train was freezing." Clarissa wandered into the lounge. "Nice colour scheme." She stood in front of the open fire warming her hands. "I see you've got the dust collectors out." Avril looked at her. "I'm only thinking of you, Avril. House cleaning is such a bind." Avril handed her mother a whiskey. "You're a godsend." She flounced over to an armchair, dragged it nearer to the fire and stuck her legs out, circling her ankles while swigging back the whiskey. "Just what the doctor ordered. Now, tell me what's going on."

Avril was glad to see her mother.

"Perhaps it's time to branch out into something else. You mentioned a cottage industry when you moved up here."

She told Clarissa about potential opportunities. "Work wants me to travel to Italy, Madrid and Germany." Avril's mother carried on slugging back her whiskey. Avril held up her glass and Clarissa nodded.

"It's up to you, but madam will be gone soon tripping the light fantastic." Avril's mother settled back into the chair, a cushion digging into the small of her back. She removed it and tossed it onto the sofa. "To be young again and all those aspirations." She looked at a black and white photograph of Avril in the alcove. "I remember when that was taken. You must have been eighteen years old." She laughed. "You were with your friend. What was her name again?"

"Photograph?" Avril frowned.

Clarissa waved her hand towards the alcove.

Avril looked across. "That's strange. I haven't seen that for ages. I thought Daniel had taken it."

Avril's mother coughed as she took another swig of the whiskey. "Jenny, that's her name. What became of her?" Avril stared at the photograph.

"She married the Martisons' son. They owned the bakery and went off to Leeds."

"Yes, I remember." Clarissa nodded. "Three children, and all in private school. She did so well for herself." She looked at Avril and shook her head in pity. "It's such a shame." Avril threw a cushion at her mother.

"I've joined the Clamount Stroud Committee run by Corenza et al," Avril announced proudly.

"WI at your age." Clarissa laughed. "Really, Avril, you're such a fuddy-duddy."

"It's about advancement of the village for the good," Avril protested.

Her mother held up her hand. "Rubbish! Don't try and convince me. A bunch of nosey parkers sticking their noses in. Just leave it and go and do something less boring instead." She stood up, stretched and grabbed the arm of the armchair to steady herself. "Some air before dinner. I'll have a look at the back garden while I'm at it too." Avril escorted her mother to the back door.

It was a cold evening. They both stepped down onto the patio.

"More manageable than your old house. I like what you've done with the climbing rose and the obelisk – now that is tasteful." Avril smiled. Her mother rarely dished out compliments. Avril rubbed her arms to stop the chill.

"The walls are original – I think seventeenth century," she said, pointing. Her mother nodded, and then took a deep breath and began coughing.

"The old lungs are adjusting from London. Goodness knows what rubbish I've breathed in." She patted her chest. "London's getting worse. Perhaps I'll move to the country." She shot a glance at Avril. Avril stood stoic.

"It's a bit chilly. I think I'll head back inside."

Clarissa took in another deep breath and coughed. "I think we'd better," she wheezed.

They moved back into the lounge, and her mother eased herself back down into the chair.

The front door slammed. Clarissa looked up.

"Casey popping out to see friends." Avril handed her mother a refill.

"This committee and Corenza, whatever her name is, and her cronies, they sound like a coven if you ask me."

"They're welcoming and kind," Avril replied, rolling her eyes.

Her mother threw her head back and laughed. The fire crackled loudly, which made Avril jump. It was then she noticed that her photograph had gone.

The next day, Avril received an urgent call from Roger, her boss, to go to Madrid. There was a problem that required her attention.

"It's only two nights. They're paying triple plus a bonus and five-star accommodation. It's a one-off," Avril explained. "Are you sure you don't mind?" Her mother shooed her towards the front door.

"Go on, you'll miss your flight. And don't worry. We'll have a blast. I may arrange an all-night rave." Avril's mother stood on the doorstep and waved as the cab disappeared up the street.

A cool blast of air pushed Clarissa back across the threshold causing her to grip the door frame. She looked up and saw a woman across the road watching. "A chill in the air!" she shouted. The blast subsided and she let go of her grip. "I'm Clarissa, Avril's mother. You must be Corenza," Clarissa called to the woman. She always pulled out the first name that came to her – that way she guaranteed she'd get the right name in response. The woman didn't reply and walked away. Clarissa watched as she was joined by another woman; they both turned and looked at her. "Nice day." A gust of wind pushed her back over the threshold again and slammed the door shut.

Avril had left her mother a list of things to do, so after breakfast, which was lashings of butter and marmalade on toast, Clarissa went sideways up the narrow staircase armed with the vacuum cleaner. She wheezed as she reached the top step. "Air." She clutched her chest on her way to Casey's room, flung open the window and took several deep breaths. "That's better." As she drew another deep breath, she could hear something. A rattling sound.

She looked at the window frame and the curtain pole but couldn't find anything causing the sound. She listened and looked towards the ceiling thinking perhaps it was a loose tile. The rattling got closer and was coming from inside Casey's bedroom. The sound appeared to come from near the chimney breast. Casey had decorated it with all sorts of colours and crystals. She walked across and looked at the pictures and arty things. *Looks like an altar*, Clarissa thought. The rattling was coming from within the chimney itself.

She steadied herself as she knelt down. Her knees and ankles clicked as she slowly leant her shoulder against the mantelpiece and put her hand just inside the lip of the chimney and felt around. Her hand made contact with something. She snatched it away and tentatively repositioned it again. She felt a small, round object and gave it a gentle pull. It came away. Slowly she extracted it and examined it more closely. It was an old-fashioned glass opaque bottle hanging from a leather strap. She gave it a gentle shake and watched a brownish slush swirl around the bottom. There was something else in the bottle: a piece of metal.

"A rusty nail and what looks like hair," Clarissa said to herself. She held it up to the light to get a better look and as she did, the window flung open and a strong gust shot across the room, causing the bottle to slip out of her hand. It smashed on the floor. A putrid smell filled the air as Clarissa ran towards the window and vomited. She then heard loud laughter.

A couple of days later, upon her return, Avril said, "This is for you. I hope you like it. And this too." She passed two pastel-coloured boxes to her mother. "Booze and something to eat." Her mother's favourite two things. "How did it go?" Avril put her luggage in the hallway and popped her head around the door into the lounge.

"Before you start, I wanted to create a space." Clarissa had moved over to the alcoves. "And you have such lovely light coming in through these small windows. And some nice flowers. I did use one of your dust collectors." She placed her hand on a vase filled with flowers. "Not quite home-grown, but near as damn it."

Avril stood by her case. "Thank you. Oh, you found my photo too!" She pointed to the black and white photograph sitting to the left of the vase. Her mother looked across.

"Oh yes, Casey's touch," Clarissa fibbed, for she hadn't noticed it.

"I'll just go and unpack and I want to put a wash on. Anything happen while I was away?" asked Avril, dragging her case up the stairs.

"No, but there's a parcel for you," her mother called from the kitchen. "I've made a stew. I hope you like it."

"Sounds nice. Parcel?" she shouted while unzipping her case.

Clarissa took out a huge earthenware casserole pot from the oven. "Yes, in the lounge." She took off the lid and used a ladle to stir the contents.

"That's odd. I wasn't expecting anything." Avril shouted as she collected a bundle of washing and headed down the staircase. As she reached midway, she lost her footing and slipped. She screamed.

Clarissa rushed to find her daughter in a heap at the bottom of the stairs and blood oozing from a cut on her forehead. "Avril!" Her mother rushed over to prop up her daughter's head. "I'll get something for the cut. Do you have any headache or dizzy spells?" Avril pulled herself up.

"No." She turned slightly to look back up the stairs. "I felt something behind me. A pressure on my back." Clarissa helped her up. "Someone pushed me. I felt a hand in the small of my back."

"Are you sure you didn't lose your footing?"

"No, it was definitely a shove." Avril shook her head. "Someone pushed me down the stairs." Clarissa looked at her.

Avril sat at the kitchen table with a hot water bottle supporting the small of her back and a shawl around her shoulders. The stew bubbled out of the large ceramic pot.

"Homemade bread too." Avril broke off a piece.

"There's plenty more. I've put some for Casey in a bowl. She can heat it up later." Her mother placed the ladle on a lazy Susan and took off her apron.

"This is nice."

Clarissa passed her the pepper mill. "I have a confession. I broke something." Avril looked at her.

"Not my Moorcroft vase." She sat up wincing. "You always hated it. I hope you didn't throw away the pieces – you know I can glue them together." Her mother shook her head.

"Thrift ever being the watchword. No, a bottle in Casey's bedroom."

Avril put down her spoon. "I've been waiting for this day." She sighed heavily. "Booze? I blame myself. You were right – I set a bad example, and there's a batch of dodgy vodka going around. I've seen reports of it on the news."

Clarissa shook her head while stirring her stew. "Let me finish, Missy Melodramatic. It wasn't alcohol. Just an old bottle stuck in the chimney breast. It may have been there for years."

"Has Casey said anything?" Avril spooned out another helping for herself.

"Not a thing," Her mother cut up a piece of bread.

"A schoolgirl prank. Probably a love potion," said Avril.

Clarissa buttered the bread. "I suspect so, or some glib fool falling for some local hooligan."

"It could have been there for years." Avril chewed on her bread. "As you said yourself, you inherit someone else's history."

"Perhaps, but there's something around this place I don't like," said her mother.

"Such as?"

Putting her elbows on the table, her mother replied, "I get shivers. I feel as though I'm being watched, and I can't sleep here."

Avril listened. Her mother may be outspoken, but she was a rational woman.

"Every night I hear the blessed sound of humming. I thought it was the fridge or that." She pointed to the central heating boiler. "A low hum – it's enough to drive you to distraction. No wonder Casey sleeps with music on."

"You can hear it, too?" asked Avril.

"And the people in the village, Avril, I sense something."

Avril felt a breeze around her neck. She shivered. Then her mother looked up. "What is it, Mother?" Clarissa looked towards the window.

"I thought I heard footsteps."

They both looked at each other. Avril shrugged and took another mouthful of stew, and then the window rattled. They both looked around; there was nothing there. Her mother sighed.

"I feel a sense of foreboding. You're new to this village, and you may have awakened something." She touched Avril's arm. "This place isn't for you. Find somewhere else." Her mother got up and put her bowl in the sink.

"I'll go and get that parcel you mentioned."

Her mother walked across and put her hand on her daughter's shoulder. "No you don't. You need to rest. I'll get it." She fetched the rectangular box wrapped in brown paper and placed it on the table.

Avril leant forward, moved the parcel closer and looked at the label, which was written in large black wavy writing and addressed to "Mistress Avril Hawksworth".

"That's weird. Who would have written to me using my maiden name?"

"It's not," said her mother, frowning.

Avril pointed to the label.

"Ms Avril Phipps," said her mother.

Avril looked again. "Oh!" She pushed the parcel to one side. "Probably something to do with work."

The three days turned into seven, and then ten before Avril was standing on the platform. She could tell that her mother was itching to get back to London.

"Thank you, Mother. We must do this more often." Avril hugged her tightly.

"Why don't you come over to stay? A change of air will do you good."

"Coughing up phlegm you mean?" Avril laughed.

Clarissa stood looking into her eyes. "The offer is there." She reached out to touch Avril's hand. "Come over in a few days. I just sense something." A tear rolled down her mother's face. She hadn't seen her mum act this way before.

"I'll come in a few weeks, but only after St Mark's Eve. I have the preparations to do."

Her mother gripped her hand harder. "Avril, I sense something. Avoid it – please leave here."

The tannoy announced the train's departure. Her mother released her grip as she ran towards the open door before the guardsman slammed it shut. Avril stood watching the train start to move faster.

"Please, Avril," she heard. "I'll call you!" Clarissa shouted.

Avril stood and waved as the train pulled away. Then a gust of wind shot around her, followed by hysterical laughter. She looked around, but no one was there.

Later that day, Casey sat staring out through the passenger window.

"How long will you be at Amber's?" asked Avril.

"One night, perhaps two. It depends," Casey replied with a shrug.

"Don't outstay your welcome, love."

"I'm sixteen – not ten." Casey looked at her. "Anyway, we're staying with her gran, and she likes the company."

Avril nodded. "Pass me the map."

Casey took her mum's phone and tapped in an address. "Next left and it's straight ahead. Only five miles." She pointed at the map on the phone, and then opened the window and reached out her arm. The traffic was bumper to bumper.

"I think everyone's leaving Clamount Stroud this weekend." Avril looked over at her daughter, who had her earphones in and was moving her head in time with the music.

The traffic lights changed and as Avril put her foot down, she saw Verity bouncing along. She beeped her horn and put up her hand.

Verity looked up and waved smiling. Casey looked at Verity in the wing mirror. Suddenly, Verity's faced changed. Her features became sharper, her arms longer and her fingers curled upwards like talons as she held up one hand and pointed laughing hysterically at Casey.

Casey screamed. Then the window suddenly closed, trapping her arm. Avril slammed on the brakes.

"Bloody idiot!" a man behind shouted as he braked hard.

"Mum! Do something!" Casey screamed, trying to pull herself free. "It's crushing my arm, Mum!"

Avril began pressing all the buttons for the windows, but nothing happened. She turned the engine over, but it failed to start. "Come on!" Avril shouted.

"Mum!" Casey screamed.

Swearing, Avril turned over the engine again and again. The car finally started.

Casey continually screamed, "My arm! Get my arm out!" She shrieked pulling at her arm wedged in the window.

Avril frantically pressed the buttons again. The window eventually went down, and Casey could now release her arm. "Let's get it checked out at A&E. It's not far."

"No! Just drop me off at Amber's!" Casey ordered, nursing her arm.

Avril could see blood on her daughter's arm. "I need to get you checked out, Casey. You may have broken it."

"No, Mum. I want to go to Amber's."

Avril could feel herself getting worked up. "Did you knock anything?" Casey shook her head, crying. "I don't understand. I pressed the button. Nothing worked." She looked at the dashboard. "It's never happened before… I just don't understand it." Avril reluctantly made her way to Amber's.

Casey put her cardigan around her arm as she got out of the car. Avril touched Casey's shoulder, but she pulled away and walked towards a young girl with flaming red hair who rushed out to greet her. Avril couldn't hear what Casey said, but her friend turned, looked and stared at her.

"The car window trapped her arm. I wanted her to go to hospital," Avril said as she walked up the pathway. "Casey, if the pain gets worse, please call me, or at least get it checked out."

An elderly woman appeared on the doorstep. "Don't you fret now. She'll be good as new. I'll apply a poultice; she'll sleep like a top." The woman smiled. A strong breeze blew against the door and the weathervane on the roof spun around. The woman stepped back. "I'd better be getting along. There's a chill in the air." She looked up at the dark clouds forming. "The devil does walk."

Avril watched the woman disappear. She walked back down the pathway as the black clouds became denser. A strong wind pushed hard against her, causing her to pitch forward. Then she heard voices.

"Mistress Hawksworth, it's not safe for thee."

She looked around, but no one was there. She looked back towards the cottage. The woman was shaking her head through the window. As Avril got back in her car, she heard her name being called: "Mistress Hawksworth, you must leave. I beg of thee." She looked again, but there was still no one around.

Clamount Stroud was undergoing a complete transformation for the St Mark's Eve celebrations as Avril drove past Spinney Fields. The sun had broken cover and it was surprisingly warm. The traffic was slow as she watched a group of workmen finish constructing a stage.

"More nails. It has to be stronger," came the distinctive voice of Mr Ouspensky, but she couldn't see him.

The traffic had come to a standstill and as well as the preparations for the celebrations, it was also market day. Vans reversed while owners dismantled their stalls, each one beeping at each other as they competed for space.

A tractor edged itself in front of her car. One of the drawbacks of country living was farm machinery. Tractors often appeared when the traffic was slow.

"You soon get to know the back lanes," she remembered Corenza mentioning.

Avril edged forward, indicated and shot down a small, narrow street. She breathed in, going around a corner with the help of a convex mirror perched on a wall. She joined the street that ran parallel to the high street, which was lined with boutique shops all with original frontage, window boxes painted in different colours, bunting that criss-crossed the street, and there was a huge sign announcing "St Mark's Mediaeval Fair".

She saw a tall man looking up admiring the sign. A car pulled out and attempted a three-point turn. It hit the kerb as it moved forward, and then hit the kerb behind as it reversed. Two men got out and exchanged raised voices. Avril sat frustrated looking at the time. She only had twenty minutes to get to the garage. She'd called ahead, and they'd booked it in.

She heard her name being called. She looked around and saw Mr Ouspensky. He waved.

"Hello, Avril, my dear. You must come and help. We need your expertise."

Avril held up her hand and smiled.

Corenza popped her head out from behind a backdrop of mediaeval peasants. "You must, Avril."

Then Pru and Verity both appeared. "We'll see you later. It will be the best St Mark's ever." They laughed.

And then there was silence before she heard the words of the elderly lady: "'Tis not safe for you, Mistress Hawksworth. You must leave. Thee must leave before St Mark's Eve."

There was no one there as she looked around her.

Avril accelerated and moved into second gear. The streamers and St Mark's celebrations extended the full length of the street and started to thin out as she headed towards the neighbouring village and to the garage. Avril had got used to the tight bends, so she increased her speed. But as she went around a corner, a dark figure was standing in the road.

She screamed and swerved, slamming on the brakes hard, causing the car to leave the road and career through some bushes. A strange smell filled the car as the air bag deployed. Avril lay slumped in the front seat.

The bright white lights hovering above made Avril's eyes flicker. She could feel herself moving and could hear the screeching sounds of wheels against a hard floor. She couldn't move. She was strapped in. Avril then felt herself being lifted upwards and placed back down again. A face looked down at her.

"You've had a lucky escape." A man shone a small torch in her eyes. "A small bleed. We'll have to get your head scanned." Avril tried to sit up but was restrained. "We needed to immobilise you in case you have a bleed or a fracture to your neck." The man gave her a mirror, which she angled upwards at the long white ceiling.

"Where am I?" Avril moved the mirror over to one side and saw a man in a black and white uniform.

"The cottage hospital in little old Clamount Stroud. We're more a hydro spa for the orthopaedics these days." He went over to a cabinet and handed her some pills. "These will help with the pain. I can give you two more in four hours, but see how you go." He put a thermometer in her mouth. "Slight concussion. Do you know how long you blacked out for?"

Avril couldn't see her watch. "Please, what time is it?"

The man angled the mirror towards a large electric clock on the wall. "It's seven p.m."

"I've been out for nearly three hours…" Avril rubbed her head. "It can't be… I remember…"

"You've had a lucky escape." The man handed her a glass with a straw. "And luckily for you, an ambulance was travelling back and saw your car." She watched the man write something on a chart. "I'm Terry by the way. Are you local?" He took hold of her wrist. Avril nodded.

"My car, it hit a tree. Something came out in front of me." She held the mirror towards the clock again. "A figure in a gown… I tried to avoid it." Terry sat on the edge of the bed.

"Don't tell matron." He laughed. "Probably a deer. They have a habit of straying onto the road and loitering."

Avril listened, but said, "It was larger. My head…" She rubbed her head again.

"Is the pain easing off?"

"Casey – I must tell her." Avril could feel tears running down her face. "My head, it hurts so much." She winced.

Terry wrote something else on her chart. "I'll come back in half an hour. If you're still in pain, I'll call through to our on-call doctor. Hopefully when we transfer you, we'll get your pain under control."

Avril watched Terry disappear. She angled the mirror sideways and could see around the rest of the ward. It was empty except for a bed in the corner. There was a bottle-green screen around. Her hands shook as she tried to get a better look. She could see that there were people behind the screen. She heard whispering, "Mistress Hawksworth," followed by laughter. Her eyes were so heavy and her arms so weak; she felt herself drift off to sleep.

Sounds of footsteps and voices stirred Avril. She opened her eyes slowly; the ward was in darkness. She felt for the mirror and angled it and could just make out that the time was 3 a.m. She could hear footsteps and voices followed by a light which now shone in her eyes. She winced seeing Terry standing over her again. Her eyes closed once more – she felt so drowsy.

"I thought you said you'd given her enough sedative," a man snapped.

"I have. It's probably involuntary movements. She can't move her body."

Avril could feel that she was being undressed. She tried to speak, but no words came out. She felt a roughness against her body, which scratched her skin, and then something tight was placed around her head.

"To protect your head," Terry whispered.

Feeling herself be lifted, she fought hard to open her eyes, but she couldn't. None of her muscles were responding. "You will open… You will open," she repeated as cracks of light appeared. She focused as hard as she could and saw Corenza, Pru and Verity. Mr Ouspensky was standing behind them.

"You gave us a fright, my dear. We thought we'd lost you." Mr Ouspensky stroked her forehead. "How are you feeling?"

Avril tried lifting her head, but it wouldn't move. She attempted to talk but no words came out.

"Hush, my dear, you're still concussed. You need to rest. We're transferring you to get the best care."

She could only look upwards as she felt her body being pushed along on a trolley down a long corridor and into a stainless steel lift. Looking upwards, she caught the reflection of herself against the sheet metal ceiling. She lay on the stretcher in a mediaeval outfit with a sign above her head: "Mistress Hawksworth".

Chanting surrounded her as she drifted off again.

"She'll be unable to move for another hour, so I suggest you get things moving as quickly as possible," Terry said as Mr Ouspensky handed him an envelope.

Avril was placed in the back of a van. She could now move her head more and looked to her side. Mr Ouspensky took her hand and held it tightly.

"We've been waiting for such a momentous occasion. This is the most wonderful day and so fortuitous for us that you came to Clamount Stroud of your own free will and with a good heart." He encased her hand and tapped it. "A direct descendant of Caleb Hawksworth."

Corenza's face moved into Avril's line of sight. "The Witchfinder." She smiled. Her face was pointed and covered in warts. "A direct descendant of the witch finder himself."

Verity's face then appeared – her face was elongated and her forehead covered in boils. "The witchfinder." She laughed. "Caleb Hawksworth do be responsible for drowning my ancestors." She placed a bunch of Scabby May onto Avril's chest.

Pru looked down. "Despicable!" she screamed. "Your Caleb Hawksworth do murder my family and drowned a babe in arms. Let your family see you suffer as we did."

They all laughed and then began chanting.

Fireworks darted and criss-crossed exploding as crowds cheered and children ran around screaming. Herds of people dressed in mediaeval costume surrounded by stalls were buying, eating, drinking and laughing. A group of musicians played instruments as an elderly man and woman danced.

"They look splendid. Would you like some, darling?" A man offered a cup of punch.

"All botanical herbs with a nice sloe gin base," a woman with blackened teeth cackled.

A procession of floats with schoolchildren dressed as urchins, sprites, ghouls and goblins circled the stage that was covered in tarpaulin.

"This is lovely. Try it – you'll like it," said Amber.

Casey took a mouthful of the pink fluffy stuff and placed it in her mouth.

"What do you think?" Amber nodded.

Fireworks crashed overhead, making Casey jump.

"It's okay" Casey said as she got out her phone. "Are you still worried about your mum?" Amber asked as she cleared her voice of the pink gunk.

"I just thought I'd see her, that's all." She looked at her phone. She'd had four missed calls from her gran.

Mr Ouspensky helped to lift Avril onto a wooden beam. "Tie her tight." His eyes were fixed on Avril's face. "She must not break free."

Avril tried to scream as she tossed her head around trying to move, and then she saw Adrian.

"You'll burn for the blight your ancestors brought on my family."

Avril cried out.

Mr Ouspensky looked at Corenza. "It's wearing off. You'll have to be quick."

They hoisted her up the beam by a pulley that slotted into the scaffolding on the stage.

Fireworks continued to explode above.

A woman stood at the side of the stage with a baton and pointed to the choir of children in front. "After three, children." As she counted, a group of youngsters dressed as goblins and ghouls came onto the stage dancing and singing.

"Ladies and gentleman," a tannoy announced, "It is now time to commence the St Mark's Eve celebrations by lighting the fire and burning the effigy to forgive the past which has blighted this community and to give thanks for the forthcoming seasons and harvest."

The tarpaulin was dropped, and Mr Ouspensky stood with the torch.

Everyone cheered at the fireworks exploding overhead, and they all watched the fire progress up the stack and to the scaffolding where the effigy hung.

Avril's screams were drowned out as Corenza, Pru and Verity danced in a circle chanting and laughing.

Casey looked towards the stage and watched the effigy burn. A cold feeling suddenly shot through her body as the smell of white musk surrounded her.

Leo

It must have been approximately six weeks ago, or maybe a little longer… yes, it could be as long as eight weeks ago when I first saw him.

I'd been rushing around doing my shopping. It was a fleeting glance at first… Yes, I remembered because my hands were hurting – the handles on the bags, one of them broke and I got myself into a real fluster. I remembered cursing the quality of the bag. I stood rubbing my hands. It was then that I caught sight of him. He was tall, I'd say over six foot three, or maybe taller, he was a similar height to Father. I could see there was a sale on, and the gaggle of women dived in like carrion crows hacking their way through flesh as they pulled, pushed and stretched the sale items. But he was polite, just smiling, looking on and taking everything in his stride.

He looked so masculine with contoured shoulders, and he wore a navy pinstriped three-piece suit, which fitted him well and accentuated his broad shoulders that tapered to his thin waist. I like men with broad shoulders. He had style and wore a red silk tie that contrasted nicely with his skin tone. He was very handsome. I tried not to make it so obvious and averted my gaze as I didn't want to appear too… well, gauche. I wondered how old he was. I'd say early thirties.

It sounds silly, but I felt all tingly. I was just being foolish – it was the loss of blood supply from that stupid bag. It cost fifty pence; and you'd have thought it would have been better quality. I gently shook my hands to encourage the blood flow to my fingers and picked up the rotten bag. For two pins I'd have gone back to the shop.

But then he saw me and smiled. I smiled back. I felt my heart racing and I became a little flustered. I hadn't expected him to see me. But he did, and he had a beautiful smile. I froze on the spot. I had to get the bus, but I remember feeling as if I were floating. I know it all sounds so stupid, but I felt happy and carefree. For God's sake, it sounds like a trashy romance novel, but I felt really uplifted.

I smiled to everyone and didn't mind being shoved or a pram hitting my calf while waiting for the bus. He had a lovely smile. I can't describe it as I've not felt it since. I'm over that now. I was happy and kept smiling.

"Lovely day isn't it?" I said to the driver as I got on. He mumbled something. I managed to get to the upper deck after squeezing past shopping bags and two thugs hogging the aisle. I still had my happy face on as I managed to hem myself into a seat at the front. I can look down into the shops as it goes along the high street. I wondered how long he'd been working there.

I didn't need to go into town for a few days, and I ended up helping Gavin with his new play. He always asks me to read the lines, which takes hours. I sat there prompting and smiling but really, I was bored. Poor Gavin, no matter what character he plays, they are all the same: wooden. He just can't put any life into his characterisation – the same hand movements and the same inflections. I'm being cruel; my mind is somewhere else. Gavin tries his best.

He's come a long way and with encouragement from his mother and me, he started going out. At first, it was just outside the house to the local shop;

and over many months, we managed to get him to travel on a bus and into town. He gradually ventured further, and that's how he stumbled into amateur dramatics. I go and watch him when he's performing and clap and cheer loudly. It makes him feel good, and it's an evening out for me too. I do wish he wouldn't address the audience, though, every time he comes on stage.

A few days later I had to go back into town to visit the bank. I don't do any of this internet banking, I don't trust it for a start; and as my local branch had closed in the village, it gave me an excuse. I try and get into town once a week. I catch the bus on the green. I do wish I'd learnt to drive. I just never had the confidence, and Father thought cars were too dangerous. I took lessons and bought driving gloves, shoes, handbag and a scarf, but I got flustered and easily distracted and veered off into the middle of the road.

I remembered going over the cat's eyes and Father grabbing the steering wheel. He was right: I was too preoccupied to drive. Besides, I love looking out on the bus as you see so much. And if I sit on the top deck, you can see right into people's homes. I got so many ideas for backdrops for the amateur dramatics. Oh yes, I volunteered my services to paint the scenery. I did A-level art and was going to art college… but my nerves. Father said it was too much, and he was right. So, I stayed at home. I wouldn't have been much good because I do like routine, and to be arty you have to be bohemian. I struggled with that as I need structure. Anyway, I couldn't cope living by myself. I've always had my parents around.

That day I thought I'd buy Father a handkerchief – something a bit special. I was thinking small polka dots in a navy; he doesn't like anything too flash. Mother always complained about washing them, but surely they're better than paper. All those tiny particles collecting in your nasal passage which travel down into the deep recesses of your lungs causing any number of problems. I always have a linen one, and it helps when I pass the bus depot. All those fumes. I hold it to my mouth and walk past choking. I decided to get Father a navy one. I thought he'd like that, and it would go well with the jacket I bought him last Christmas.

The bus was taking the more scenic route. I realised I'd caught the 128. No matter, I wasn't in a rush and it goes through Quinton. It's not bad and there are some nice executive houses. I often dream of owning my own house. Mother thought it would be too much of a burden. All the bills and the upkeep and the cooking too. Yes, she's right. I struggle now with helping Mother and Father. They don't get around so much these days, but the cleaning is exhausting. I do love the house on the corner. It has the most wonderful colour scheme.

I often get lost daydreaming. When I was at school I would gaze out of the window. I remembered Miss Catlow throwing a piece of chalk at me. It's strange when you're younger dreaming of your life and what may lie ahead. So many girls always talked of marriage, children, a house which they'd clean weekly and going on holidays. For some reason none of that appealed. I knew I would remain single. I often wondered if your life is predetermined as I've never had many relationships.

It was busy in town. I had to walk virtually against the shop windows as mothers with their children three-deep hogged the pavement. I really wished they'd be more considerate. I don't mind children, but it's the mothers with their sense of self-entitlement. It must be something triggered as soon as they give birth; they are just so self-centred. And the weight, many of them waddle around like ducks – they must have magic mirrors at home. They let their children run around causing pandemonium. No wonder there are so many serial killers around.

Oh no, I got caught up in a cloud of anger, things whirling around my mind, the injustice of it all, and then I was outside. My heart was thumping again. It was ridiculous. I was only going in to browse. He might not even have been there, let alone remembered me. I decided to poke my head in and take a look.

Oh my Goodness! He was there! He was wearing a charcoal bluish-grey suit that day. It was a really nice fit and a good quality cloth. He looked like the men you see in gyms and who appear on the cover of health magazines. His hair was swept back, greased at the sides, black with a beautiful sheen.

My feet wouldn't move. I felt so silly, so girly, and then two women pushed past deep in conversation, so I tagged behind them and followed. They headed down the aisle to the formal suit hire section. I started to laugh. One of the women turned and looked at me. I looked down pretending to giggle at a label. *I'm so glad people can't read my thoughts.* I headed to towards the wedding section.

Was this irony or had I set the intention and there was a message? I just couldn't stop giggling. I riffled through my bag pretending to look for something, a mobile phone perhaps, even though I don't possess one. I headed down another aisle and was faced with boxer shorts and pants. I felt so embarrassed. One of the sales assistants made a beeline for me. I turned and rushed down to formal wear. I couldn't see him, but what would I have said if I had? I'd gone red, that's what would have happened. I wish I didn't blush, get a dry throat and talk gibberish when I'm embarrassed.

I took a sharp left and went down to the rails of jackets. I fondled the material, which was cashmere and very sensual. I love a man in a nicely cut jacket. I looked around and saw him! My hands were trembling as I looked down at the jacket again pretending to examine it in more detail. I wondered whether he'd spotted me. I looked up and saw him smiling. I smiled back and shot my gaze back to the jacket. *I'll edge down another aisle looking down – yes, that's what I'll do.* I could hear voices, and one of the other assistants was standing next to him. He was patting him on his shoulder and, oh, I heard him being called Leo. That is a lovely name. I absolutely adore that name, so middle-class too.

There was a group of women hovering, and so obvious. One of them thrusted her bosoms out – they were probably silicon given the size of them! Leo, he just took it in his stride; I could see he wasn't interested. Why would he want a woman made of plastic? I looked up again, and he smiled at me. I looked away and then caught my reflection in the mirror, I didn't look bad. My hair looked good, my make-up applied nicely, not rushed, it was even and natural. I looked up once more, and he looked at me again and smiled.

Those bloody women were fussing over him demanding attention. I felt so angry I could have screamed. I thought that I'd have to pop in later or another day but would announce my departure first. I decided to go past and look up. It wouldn't have been right to just go without leaving a lasting impression. I casually walked down the aisle, my jacket fully open exposing my tiny waist and ample bosom. I stopped and laughed to myself as I remembered I was walking back to the wedding section.

I often planned for my marriage. I'd kept a bottom drawer ever since I was twelve. Nana gave me things, and I inherited bits and pieces from an elderly aunt, plus I had money saved up in a building society account. I had quite the bottom drawer, but for some reason or other it hadn't gone to plan. Mother was right about marriage being overrated, and my life was full. I looked after my parents and made birthday cards and was quite busy in the spare bedroom ensuring my card making was quite profitable. Ironically, my marriage cards were bestsellers. Many remarked on the lovely romantic scenes and verses. I love writing verses.

I was still laughing as I passed Leo. He looked at me. His eyes were so vibrant and the smile... His whole face lit up. He was going to approach, I could tell, but the other assistant needed him, waving swatches of fabric near him while the women swooned. As I crossed the threshold, I looked over my shoulder and then did a double take. Leo had noticed. He smiled back at me!

The bank was busy, and I had to queue up for ages. A woman in front complained about the lack of staff.

She was right. There was one counter staff, and they'd installed a whole raft of automatic counter service machines. I watched people queuing at them. One man was banging the keys and swearing. Another complained that it was rejecting the money he was trying to pay in. And me, well, I had a stack of cheques to pay in. The old dears like writing cheques and they never carried money. Some were only for a pound, but it was a steady income. I earn extra from doing calligraphy and I even wrote a book, self-published of course, but at least I'm leaving a footnote of my life.

The cashier was getting frustrated and shouting at an elderly woman. Poor dear, she was hard of hearing. Why do people shout at people who are deaf? I don't understand customer service these days – everyone is so angry.

I didn't mind waiting; I could lose myself in my thoughts. Leo's trousers had razor-sharp creases. I would never be able to get creases like that even if had one of those super-duper steam irons similar to the one in the laundrette. I wondered if he was spoken for. He didn't look attached. He looked vulnerable. That smile – I could tell he was not with someone. He needed someone to look after him. I wondered if he lived with his parents. I think he did; he looked sensitive. I wondered what food he liked. It's silly really, I should make more of an effort to cook. I do like plain food, though, but I make one of the best gravy dinners around.

The old lady had finished being served and the cashier looked frazzled. She was hoarse, and I could hear her making nasty comments. She'd left the hearing loop on and her voice was echoing. "Silly bitch," she said and tutted when I handed in the paying in slip and several cheques. She pointed to the machines. I looked at her and asked whether she could do it for me. She wasn't having a good day. That's the beauty about getting older: you can become indifferent, and it comes very easily these days.

I had to walk past Leo's shop again. I thought I would look in the window – they always had a nice display and I could linger longer. It was a warm day, so I took my jacket off. My arms are quite toned. I do a lot of gardening and so many chores around the house. It's amazing how people just don't realise that there's no need for gyms: lifting, pulling, pushing and digging keep you in shape. I used to wear a cardigan as Mother didn't like muscles on a woman.

I saw Leo; he was standing in the middle of the shop floor. He looked uncomfortable. It must be agony being on your feet standing all day. I hoped he was having sufficient breaks. I noticed that his trousers tapered, showing his ankles. He had nice ankles. Most men can't carry them off as they normally have fat, hairy ankles, but his were slim and tanned. He was wearing a different jacket. That's the bonus of working in a fashion shop – you get to wear the merchandise and can change throughout the day. I wondered what was going on in his head as he stood there helping customers. I thought he must have a lot of patience. I could tell when I first saw him. He didn't rush to anyone and he smiled. He was single – I could feel it. He didn't have a ring on his finger. I tried to remember which was the marriage hand on a man. I always get confused. No, he was single, I was sure. I felt relieved.

Leo was shy. I could see that a woman had gone up to him. He said few words, but smiled. They had sales baskets just inside the door, so I thought I'd pop in and browse. He'd surely see me again. But I paused - twice in one day – does that constitute stalking? No, I'm was passing and… Besides they were new sales items out which I bet Leo put out to entice me in so we could finally talk to each other. I would go in. No, it would look too desperate.

I plucked up the courage to look through the sales items. Socks, they were quite nice. The jackets were either extra small or extra-large. It must be nice to be able to fit into sales items. I stayed a few more minutes as my bus wasn't due for another twenty minutes. I couldn't look again – it was too much. I decided to slip away. Leo was preoccupied with a man, but I felt his penetrating blue eyes as I steeled away and a warm feeling came over me. I was sure he was accessing my innermost thoughts. I wanted to go back, introduce myself and ask for his help. I took a deep breath, turned and marched back to the shop and through the door, but Leo wasn't there. My eyes darted around until I saw him in the corner with a group of sales assistants. They were all laughing, and one of them had his hand on Leo's shoulder. I bowed my head and left.

When I got home that evening, I stood gazing at my reflection. A wave of melancholy came over me and for a brief moment I could see my younger self getting ready to go out. I was wearing a new fitted dress which looked so nice. I was going out with Ben. Mother had done my hair and allowed me to wear her watch – it had diamantés and shimmered in the light. I had on a new bolero jacket too, which I'd bought from the catalogue. Father asked me to give him a twirl as I laughed. I looked so pretty and slender. I was standing at the window looking out for

Ben for over an hour. Father made excuses about the roads and cars being so unreliable. Mother thought that maybe he'd got caught up at work. Surely he would phone. I waited for three hours. I remember taking off my make-up and reluctantly hanging up my dress. I never saw Ben again. I suppose that's when things started to change, when I began to go into myself. But I knew something was different this time.

I wiped a tear from my eye and smiled as I removed the last remnants of my make-up. I could see Leo standing beside me. His hands were soft as they touched my neck. I closed my eyes and I could smell his cologne when his lips made contact with the nape of my neck. I moved over to the bed and got in; I could still feel him around me. I pulled up the bolster cushion and felt Leo's body, the warmth of his naked flesh as he drew his muscular arms around holding me tight.

Catastrophe struck. I came down with the rotten flu. I had hot and cold sweats and shivered. I just couldn't keep warm. I remember lying in bed looking out of the window too weak to get up. I heard voices outside, but I just couldn't move. Mother and Father were too frail to help. They would, I know, but I'd be all right. It wouldn't last long.

I lay looking at the magnolia tree. I remember Father planting it when I was a girl. How it had grown. It was only a couple of feet then; now it was over thirty feet or more. And there was such activity. Robins and blue tits would dart around from tree to tree avoiding the cat from next door, which lay waiting in the long grass. A squirrel would jump and helter-skelter down the trunk and run along to the bird bath. I saw a couple of wood pigeons on a branch. It snapped and the stupid things fell to the ground. The cat swooped, but luckily they managed to take off just in time. They are so thick. I decided I'd go into the kitchen later and make myself some soup.

A few days later, I was much stronger and got up out of bed. I did a few things around the house. Mother liked the place tidy, so I dusted and sifted through all the letters. So much junk mail – all those menus. I put a sign on the letterbox "No Junk Mail", but every day something came through. I thought I'd better respond to a couple of letters, and then pop round to see Gavin, he'd be worried, and the next day I thought I might go into town. Yes, I'd go into town. I wondered whether Leo had missed me. It had been nearly two weeks. I hadn't realised the flu would take hold for so long, but there you go, these things happen. Perhaps he'd gone on holiday. The weather was warmer, and he'd probably gone to top up his tan. Yes, I would go into town tomorrow.

As I needed to get into town earlier because I had quite a bit to do, I caught the 126 which was direct. I was behind with my card making but had made up some the previous night. There was a baby shower. I wondered why they called it that. Plus, Mrs Barnes was retiring. She wanted me to make her invitations. I'd had to go to the stationery shop because I needed good quality paper – you can't buy it at the usual newsagents. And, of course, Leo. I knew I had to make time for him.

I was deep in thought about a new verse I could write when the bus jolted and the driver shouted at someone. I looked up to see that the high street was closed. There were signs everywhere announcing the layout of new water pipes, and they'd built a web of ramps and footbridges into each of the shops. It looked a right bomb site. I wondered how Leo was coping with this disruption. And the dust! It was everywhere as workmen cut into stone. I coughed and my eyes started to run. I was worried I was going to look a state.

I decided to get off at the first bus stop because it would have taken too long to get to the bus station. Tempers were fraying as people pushed and shoved, and then I felt one of the seams on my sleeve rip. I got off and looked at the hole under my arm. I looked like I'd been dragged through a bush backwards. I was so angry. I removed my jacket and carried it over my arm while attempting to go around the hurdles and ramps.

Suddenly, I went over on my ankle and pain shot up my leg. I limped to the side to rub my ankle and watched people jostle past. I continued up the high street in the direction of Leo's shop. I paused outside and caught my reflection. I quickly reapplied some make-up but the pain in my ankle was unbearable. I wasn't going to limp. I wouldn't give in to petty mishaps. I took a deep breath and headed into the shop. I decided I'd go up to Leo and ask him for his assistance. *They say fortune favours the brave.*

Glancing around the shop, I realised it looked different. The layout of the interior and the decoration had all changed. On the far wall, which had been painted a light lemon, there was now a garish burgundy wallpaper, which made me feel nauseous. The stock had changed, too. Gone was the formal section; instead, there was a whole area on a nautical or "New England" theme. They had flashes of colour for the children's section – I couldn't remember that before. There was even a home department with scatter cushions and rugs. The New England theme continued there, too. The whole shop was different.

I recognised one of the sales assistants, but I couldn't see Leo. I walked down each of the aisles, which were wider, and the carpet was now laminate. All I could hear was the sound of my shoes. Where was Leo? There was a huge beach display over one side. Perhaps he was working over there. I rushed past, but nothing. There was an upstairs, which I hadn't seen before. I saw a sign for formal wear pointing up a flight of stairs. I smiled in relief. That was where Leo would be.

My ankle throbbed. One of the sales assistants suggested I take the lift. I refused. When I reached the top step, my limp was more pronounced and I was breathless. I looked around holding onto the balustrade. I couldn't see Leo. I walked down each of the aisles, but I just couldn't find him. I thought perhaps it was his day off or he'd gone away. He'd probably gone on holiday, it was that time of year. I decided to ask, so rehearsed what I would say. "Excuse me, I'm a friend of Leo's. Is he in today?" I thought that sounded convincing and decided I'd go up to one of the sales assistants and ask. But my throat felt restricted, and I knew gibberish would come out. I felt sick; the room began to spin. I couldn't breathe.

A couple stared at me as I pushed by. I could feel my legs turning to jelly. I was going to fall, I could feel it. I slumped forward and my chest felt tight. A shop assistant rushed over and offered me a chair. I refused. I needed to get out of the shop. He took me to the lift, I just couldn't manage the stairs, and he helped me to the door. I protested I'd be all right.

Then, without thinking, I just asked, "Where is Leo? I'm a friend. I need to see him. I have a message."

The man stared and apologised as he didn't know a Leo, and then he asked whether I had the right shop. Maybe I was mistaken. I thought that must be it. He said something else, but everything was so woolly. I just couldn't hear clearly.

Feeling very sick, I just ran. I could hear the man calling after me. Perhaps they thought I was a shoplifter. I ran into the street and just kept running, my ankle hurt so much, but I kept going until I turned a corner.

I staggered to a nearby coffee shop and sat in a window seat. I just didn't know what was happening. I took some tablets out of my handbag. They help me when I become overwhelmed. Why didn't I speak to Leo when he was so obviously interested in me? I knew he was going to approach me. Those damn women. Damn, damn women! I thumped my fist on the table. A young man and women looked over. Bugger them, I was in distress. Perhaps I needed to go back to the shop. I didn't explain myself… I didn't explain… I just didn't know… I was all confused.

I thought perhaps they had dismissed him. But they wouldn't have dismissed him; he was too good. The shop had changed, so perhaps he'd got a new job. I felt so silly – he was probably taking annual leave because he couldn't do with all the fuss. And that shop assistant, what did he know? He'd probably only started that week. I laughed. Of course he was on holiday. Leo was on holiday. Yes, he was away.

I went to the stationery shop, where my mood elevated. They had a special offer, and I bought quite a few things. I must have spent over fifty pounds, but I knew I'd soon make it back. I had invites and menus to prepare for Mrs Hirst's granddaughter's wedding in a few weeks. I laughed again. Why did marriage keep coming up in conversation? It was so silly.

I cut through one of those side alleys past the cinema that runs parallel with the shops on the high street. My ankle felt better, things were running past my head, and I could hear my shoes echoing against the cobbles, they were making an empty hollow sound.

I must have walked a hundred, perhaps a hundred and fifty feet, and then I stopped at a small clearing. I was at the back of the shops. I rarely walked down the side alley as Mother thought it too dangerous, and Father preached to me regularly that rapists hide in dark corners. I could see a skip at the back of the shop, which they must have been using to dispose of all the old furnishings. I moved closer and saw the old rails and display cabinet. They looked too good to throw out. I saw a group of men carry stuff and toss it into the skip. I stood watching and then something caught my eye.

At first I wasn't sure. I walked forward very slowly, and then I saw him. It was... It was Leo. I dropped my bags and was about to run but I didn't want to make myself look silly. The men went in and Leo was standing there. He'd been drafted in to help. Poor love having to do that manual work. He wasn't even dressed for it.

I rushed across and he stood smiling. I went up to him and began talking. He just kept beaming as we talked. The conversation flowed easily. I then went on about my card business and before I knew it, I'd blurted out that I had steak and would he like dinner that evening? Everything moved so quickly. Yes, I could get a cab home and he would join me. I had to pinch myself.

The cab driver made such a fuss. I don't know why. Leo was tall, but surely cab drivers can't discriminate. It was a wonderful journey. I wouldn't shut up. I reminded myself I should remember to give him the opportunity to respond and not cut across him.

The dinner was wonderful. I had a nice red wine and all the vegetables were beautiful, too. Leo loved steamed vegetables. He went to the gym and, yes, he could stay the night. I didn't see why not. My mother and father wouldn't mind. These are modern times and besides, they liked to see me happy. Yes, I could see Mother smiling with approval and Father agreeing as I gave them both a light dusting. The matching vases do look nice; I couldn't bear the thought of scattering their ashes.

I helped Leo into the lounge as he felt a little woozy. It must have been all that wine and those long hours. I made up the spare bedroom, put the chain on the front door and pulled the curtain across to block out the draft. I didn't want Leo catching a cold.

Leo looks good in Father's suit, and he enjoys sitting by the fire. I feel so happy seeing Leo's lovely smile as we sit here each evening.

Mind you, I'll have to get something for his leg. We'd easily patch that up. I've got some glue, which works well on plastic.

Trapped

The Towers stood on the edge of the park and if you walked by, you couldn't fail to notice the neoclassical facade and Corinthian columns. The unsuspecting eye would conclude it was a majestic home occupied by old money or someone self-made, but as you moved closer you would see the ivy smothering the front of the once-occupied balconies, the white rendering flaking off exposing damp walls, the stained-glass windows, which dominated the south side of the house, suffocated with reinforced opaque glass, and the grounds besieged with rambling rhododendron bushes covering the once finely manicured lawns. The former award-winning rose beds lay euthanised under carcasses of bed frames and chairs, and as you moved to the front, laurel bushes prevented inquisitive eyes from peering too closely at the occupants of The Towers. Large signs dotted around the perimeter warned any trespassers of the consequences if they were found in the grounds and listed a number of disclaimers to those permitted to enter. The Towers pedigree had been relegated to that of a residential care home.

It was a warm evening, so a door of the French windows on the ground floor was lodged open abandoning any sense of safety, the calico curtains gently caressing the rotten wooden frames. If you listened closely, you could hear the muffled sounds of seventies music interspersed with the whirling of oscillating fans circulating warm, humid air laced with disinfectant.

A shadow stood on the marble step by the French windows looking into a large room containing four hospital beds. A faded Afghan rug sat in the middle of the room secured with tape, which masked the holes in the linoleum that revealed an unpolished parquet floor. At the far end, a woman rested her head in her hands as she sat at a small regulation standard teak-effect desk. A breeze circulated causing her to stir. She rubbed her eyes and looked up at the dark figure standing directly in front of her holding a bag.

"Oh, you scared me!" The woman shot up, slipped on her shoes and adjusted her hair. "You're from the agency?" The man nodded slowly, his face obscured by shadow. "I wasn't asleep… I was practising my mindfulness meditation and must have…" She riffled through a pile of magazines and pulled out a book. The man moved closer.

"The front door was ajar." He spoke in a low, melodic voice.

"Oh, somebody must have popped out to their car." She adjusted her uniform, pulling out the creases. "I'm Fiona, the deputy night manager. Are you the SRN?" The man stared and slowly nodded. "I'm so pleased. We've been struggling to find anyone to come here."

A chill filled the air as he stepped out of the shadows illuminated only by the lamp light. "I'm Dominic, Dominic van Sant," he said slowly. His large blue eyes locked onto Fiona. His skin was iridescent, changing under the light, and the chill intensified as he moved closer.

Stepping back, Fiona grabbed a cardigan from the back of the chair before switching off the fan.

"A locker?" He held up a battered leather bag.

Fiona looked at the oblong bag, which reminded her of Dr Protector who used to carry one when she was doing her training. She pointed to a cupboard. "Over there. It doesn't lock, but it will be safe. Just be careful of the floor." She pointed down to the floorboards fixed with masking tape. "We had a gas leak and they had to cap off the supply. The whole place is a deathtrap."

She looked up at Dominic, but he was gone. She looked around and saw him standing over one of the beds at the far side of the room. Fiona hurried across, her shoes squeaking on the floor.

"Roxy, she's eighty-nine and fit as a fiddle, but she's away with the pixies most of the time." She looked down at the grey-haired woman clutching a teddy bear. "A real beauty in her time. Foxy Roxy as she was known." Fiona shook her head. "Poor love, she's doubly incontinent and whiffs a bit." She waved her hand across her face while walking over to another bed. "We have Marianne, Elsie and there is Frances over there with the patchwork quilt." Fiona stood awkwardly. "They shouldn't be too much trouble. They've all had their medication. If you follow me." She looked at her watch. "I'll be finishing in thirty minutes, so if we can continue the handover."

There was a loud bang and the grey cupboard door swung open, spewing papers out across the floor.

"Oh no!" She rushed across and grabbed at the documents as they flew around like confetti. She waved her arms about scooping them up and shoving them back inside, and then she pushed her body hard against the cupboard door. "I must get John to fix this sodding lock."

Hysterical laughter filled the room. She looked around, but all she could see was Dominic standing over Marianne and he appeared to be whispering something to her. She walked back over towards him.

"That's Marianne. A former teacher. She never married." She paused and leant towards Dominic. "She had a companion – a female."

A cold chill made her retreat quickly. Dominic looked up, and she noticed his eyes. They seemed different, greenish. She shuddered as a cold chill dispersed around her.

"They said it was going to be one of the warmest evenings." She went over to the French windows, kicked the foot stool away and closed the door.

The lamp flickered and began to fade, creating shadows along the walls. Fiona rushed over to the teak-effect desk as the shadows followed. She felt someone tap her on the shoulder. She turned, but no one was there. The shadows hovered while she fiddled with the lamp switch, which was stuck.

"For God's sake," she said to herself.

The shadows moved closer. She tried both hands, her knuckles going white under the strain. A bright white light shot out from under the shade, causing her to stumble backwards.

"Shit!"

Loud laughter filled the room.

"Who's laughing?" She looked round, but Dominic wasn't there. She looked up towards the ceiling. "Must be coming from the men's section."

Fiona adjusted the light and saw Dominic standing by another bed. She walked across, the shadows following her.

"That's Elsie." She looked around and saw the shadows lurking by the grey cupboard. "She was a housewife, lived for her children and grandchildren." Fiona watched the shadows as they retreated. She moved over to the French windows and pulled the curtains. "She has Lewy body dementia. And we have Frances here," she added, walking over to the bed in the corner. "A charity do-gooder and always eager. A really sad story. An academic in her time, one of these revolutionary people, women's liberation I think." She paused watching the shadows again. "She retired early and did a lot for the local community, and she was going to the train station to pick somebody up, probably to run them around – she was always doing that – but she tripped and hit her head on the platform, which resulted in a slow bleed and ended up causing..." Fiona shook her head. "Poor love – not long now."

She pulled the blanket up on the bed. A cold chill came across her and as she looked up, she saw Dominic standing next to her. She walked back over to the French windows to check the door, but it was still closed. She balanced on tiptoe to close the side windows, and then heard voices followed by laughter.

"Sorry, did you say something?" She turned and looked over at Dominic, but he'd moved to another bed. He looked at Fiona and stared. His eyes were much darker.

"Perhaps it was the radio," he suggested, placing his hand on Frances's shoulder.

"Radio? There isn't one," she said slowly. "The management won't pay for one. We're lucky we've got electricity!" She looked at her watch, "I really need to be going shortly. I'll show you down to the kitchen. Edwin can give you the tour upstairs of the men's section." She turned and walked across the room, stumbling over the edge of the rug. She muttered while slamming her heel down on the mat, but it came unstuck again when she walked over to the door.

Dominic followed as Fiona led him down a long screed corridor, her shoes squeaking. She stopped and took off her cardigan.

"Goodness, it's sweltering."

The warm, clammy air circulated with the help of two bronze oscillating fans fastened to the walls, which caused paperwork on the cork noticeboard to flutter. The strip lighting flickered overhead.

"I don't know what's going on today. First the temperature and now the electrics." She fanned herself with her hand. She looked around at Dominic, but he'd gone. As she turned in the direction of the kitchen, she saw him standing there. "I see you've found the most important place. You can make yourself a cuppa here. The geezer is kept on all the time, so the water should be piping hot. If it gets cold, just switch off and on here." She pointed to a socket with a sign warning not to switch it off. "It's temperamental like the rest of the place. Just look at the ceiling." She looked up at the discoloured polystyrene tiles hanging down clinging to the last remnants of glue. "Just one spark and the place would go up. Oh, this is Edwin."

A small man with thick, dark hair and a low hairline stood looking up at Dominic. "Hiya, buddy. Welcome to the madhouse. This is Nesta."

"Oh, hi, babes. Are you all right, hon?" Nesta waved her arm. She was covered in tattoos, had a piercing through her nose and her hair was dyed purple. "Babe, you've met the 'old dears', 'ave you? That Roxy is a one." Nesta laughed. She moved closer to Dominic, but a cold rush of air pushed her back. "Bloody hell." She looked up. "She's mad as a box of frogs. She's always trying to kick her legs up."

Ed held his nose. "She's a bit smelly." Nesta and Ed looked at one another and smirked.

"Edwin, don't say that." Fiona raised her eyebrows and looked in Dominic's direction. "Sorry, but it's been a long day." She looked at her watch. "Dominic, I'll be leaving in five minutes. I'll just show you the medical cabinet and the paperwork. Nesta and Edwin will also be leaving within the next hour. I'm just going to spend a penny. Edwin, be a love and show Dominic around the men's section." She hurried down the corridor. Ed watched Fiona disappear.

"Useless cow. If I ran the place, I'd have them all on 'do not resuscitate'. What's the point of keeping the poor dabs hanging on? It's unfair."

"It's cruel." Nesta nodded. "They've had their life; they should give them something." She poured herself a mug of hot water out of the geezer and dunked a teabag.

Ed leant against the wall and said, "I'll be glad to get out of this place. It's so boring. I want excitement. I don't like being stuck with a bunch of oldies. I wouldn't let myself get into such a state. I'd rather die a quick death me." He laughed.

Just then, a cold chill blasted Ed in the face, causing him to stumble backwards into boxes of incontinence pads.

"You okay, babe?" Nesta helped him up.

"I hates this place, I do." He rubbed the dirt off his uniform. "I'll sue the management." He took a sip from his mug. "What agency are you from, buddy?" The lights dimmed. Dominic stood in the shadows, his eyes darker.

"Guardian Personnel," he said slowly.

"Not heard of that one."

"Nor me," Nesta said, shaking her head. She opened a packet of cigarettes and offered one to Ed.

"So many agencies around these days and most of them crap." Ed looked at Dominic. "I mean the dodgier ones. No offence like." He lit a cigarette for himself and Nesta.

"I love my fags." Nesta wafted the smoke with her hands. "Press mute on the panel, love." She pointed to a large metal cabinet on the wall that encased the fire alarm panel.

Ed pressed the button. An orange light flashed and announced, "Alarm held."

"How long have you been nursing?" Ed asked, blowing smoke upwards. He aimed for one of the dislodged polystyrene tiles. "I'll have it next time." He gave a throaty cough.

Dominic stood listening. Ed continued talking.

"Me, I would get a nice motor and start up a good residential home. The type for the rich. They'd pay anything if they know they're getting good service." He flicked the ash on the floor. "Right, buddy, I'll show you upstairs. Nesta and me will be shooting off for a couple of pints."

Nesta nodded. "We need it after a shift in this hellhole." She took a puff of her cigarette and tossed the ash into a mug.

Dominic followed Ed up a wide set of stairs flanked by intricate sculptured balustrades painted grey and two bronze fans screwed to the architrave oscillating the warm, clammy air. Ed stood in front of a large room.

"Bert to your right. He keeps himself to himself. If he stirs he'll probably go on about Bobby. That was his dog. Tell him he's out in the garden. The poor sod had to be put down as he couldn't look after him." Ed winced at the smell of pee. "His catheter must have come out." He pulled the sheets back and pushed the tube back into his urethra.

Bert cried out. Ed then handed Dominic a sheet of paper.

"Where are we? Yep, Bert, Alf, Steel, the champion weightlifter, and Ralph. They shouldn't be any problems as I give them diazepam, so that usually keeps them knocked out till the morning. Mind you, Steel can get up in the night. Nothing seems to knock him out, so if I were you, I'd check on him every hour just to make sure. If he does get up, just give him extra diazepam." Ed stood looking over Steel. "He was your original hunk, but look at him now – skeletal. He hasn't got long, poor bugger." He walked over to a cabinet by Steel's bed and poured a milky substance into a syringe and put it in the side of Steel's mouth. Ed looked around. "There you are. You move fast, buddy."

Dominic was leaning over Bert whispering something to him.

"That's nice, a bedtime story?" Ed laughed before a cold blast shot him backwards. "What the…?" He grabbed the side of the bed and walked over towards Dominic. "Bloody fans. We care about our patients and go the extra mile." He looked towards Dominic and winked. "The doc says it's okay to increase the meds. It's kind that way." Ed moved over to the French windows and flung them open. "Plenty of fresh air is good." He stood on the balcony, lit another cigarette and looked back at Dominic. "You don't look like a nurse. More like—" he laughed "—someone more formal. The suit type." He continued laughing. "To be honest, buddy, you could pass as a bloody undertaker. You have that way about you." He drew hard on his cigarette looking upwards to the stars, slowly blew out smoke rings and laughed to himself.

Dominic watched Ed stand on the edge of the balcony. The guard rail wobbled as he leant over. Ed took another drag on his cigarette.

"I'd love to live in one of those big houses over there, buddy." Ed pointed across the park to the rows of lights coming from the large houses. The sounds of laughter and music could be heard. "They're always having big parties, and the cars." He leant forward, his arms resting on the wrought-iron rail. "I walk past them when I come to work. What a life." He turned and winked at Dominic. "Right, I'm out of here." He flicked his cigarette ash over the balcony.

Fiona was standing by the large front door. "I'm off. I'll see you all on Tuesday. Bye, Dominic. Edwin, just do a final check on the ladies and complete the handover to Dominic." Fiona stumbled over the threshold as she slammed the door. "This place!." She walked across the uneven flagstones and as she reached the carpark, her car alarm went off.

"Come on my, loves." Edwin moved over to Roxanne and repositioned her sheet. "Oh, there is a beauty. Look at those beautiful legs... scrawny as hell." He laughed while tucking her in.

"He's so cruel. I love it." Nesta laughed, too.

Ed then moved across to Marianne. "You old lesbo." He chuckled as he moved the buzzer out of reach. He walked over to Elsie. "Your daughters never visit." He turned to Dominic. "They have power of attorney and sold her house and been on world cruises. When was it they last visited?" he whispered in Elsie's ear. "She can't hear – deaf as a post. Those two useless fat heifers of your daughters both bleeding you dry. Oh yes… they visited three months ago. So busy – busy living in their massive houses. And you in some dingy-run care home." He laughed again. "They even asked whether there was anywhere cheaper to put you! That's your loving daughters for you."

"He kills me he does." Nesta giggled.

Frances, another resident, lay staring upwards at a fly caught in one of the glass globe lights trying desperately to escape. She watched it try to walk to the top of the globe, but it fell back down. The fly repeated the same actions time and time again. It was trapped, destined to die a slow, lingering death.

Ed was now scrawling some notes on a chart. "There's an emergency number. It will take you to the deputy service. They take ages to answer, so I wouldn't bother if I were you, but just in case one of our old dears decide to kick the bucket, we have to be seen to be ticking the boxes," he said with a wink. "Right, that's me. A quick slash and I'm out of here. Do you have any questions? They'll be no bother." He walked up to Dominic and placed a hand on his shoulder, but a blast of cold air pushed him backwards. "What the…?" He looked towards the French windows, but they were closed. He walked down the corridor. Muffled voices and laughter followed him, and someone pushed him, causing him to stumble. "Bloody hell!" He got up and grabbed his coat and bag.

"Wait for me!" Nesta shouted. She ran after him and slammed the front door behind them.

Dominic took his bag out of the locker, placed it in the centre of the room and opened the clasps. Walking over to the nurses' station, he sat down, took a deep breath and slowly moved his head around while humming. The lighting dimmed and the French windows opened. A soporific feeling filled the room along with a warm breeze.

Paperwork on the desk began moving, softly at first, before gently cascading to the floor, curling and undulating across the rug and into the direction of the French windows and out onto the patio and across the lawn. All the cabinets opened at once and their contents catapulted through the air and out through the French windows. Dominic continued to hum a low, melodic tone and as he did so, an orange light slowly rose out of the bag. The light became more intense as it filled the room, and Dominic's humming became louder. The trapped fly eased its way out of the globe and flew around the room and then out through the window.

Then, the room plunged into darkness and Dominic stopped humming.

A small green speck of light tumbled in through the French windows and landed on the Afghan rug. It slowly grew, engulfing the room with iridescent colours of green, indigo, orange and blue. Dominic's eyes glowed green under the spectrum of colours as he began slowly whispering words and then repeating them.

A white orb rose up from the floor and onto the desk. Dominic seized the glowing sphere and stared into it intensely. His face glowed as he looked over at Roxy, then to Frances, Marianne and Elsie. His lips moved as he repeated his mantra; he moved his head around in circles rhythmically with the orb illuminating his face.

He breathed in deeply and slowly looked up. He continued to move his head in a musical motion as his voice went up through the ceiling towards Ralph, Steel, Alf and Bert. He then moved his head gently from side to side repeating other words as the colours became more vibrant, filling the room and penetrating the ceiling. Pink light filled the corridors and rushed up towards the men's section before enveloping all the occupants.

The warm breeze and the crackling sound of a radio intensified as the crescendo of humming and whispering increased. The sounds vibrated the inner ears of the women and men, travelling deep into their subconscious. Flashes of light flickered across their eyes as a rainbow of light bounced across the beds and walls.

"The door," Dominic said softly. "Imagine you are standing in front of a door, and watch carefully as it slowly opens and see the colours. Red, orange, yellow and the glowing around you." A radio played crackly jazz music. A saxophone sound filled the room as everything went deathly quiet. A solo saxophonist walked down the corridor, the sound of the instrument echoing all around.

A young woman rose up where Roxanne lay and stood looking around the room. A woman in a tweed jacket and skirt sat on the edge of Marianne's bed. A woman with a bun sat where Elsie was lying. And a woman stood with a coat and a bag reading a list where Frances had been sleeping. She tapped her foot on the floor.

"Ladies, where are we going tonight?" Roxy looked at herself in the mirror. "I feel like celebrating and perhaps there'll be a couple of dishes out tonight." She laughed. "I fancy myself a spiv. One with a fast car where I can feel the wind through my raven tresses." She spun around, her dress undulating.

Looking over her glasses, Marianne asked, "Shouldn't you be studying, my dear?"

Roxy wet her lips gazing at her reflection in the mirror. "I will be, my dear. The male of the species is my forte," she replied, laughing. "Remember, men seldom make passes at girls who wear glasses." She blew her a kiss.

Marianne shook her head and continued to read her book.

"We will have to make sure the children have got all their food and drink," Elsie said, brushing some lint off her blouse. "We must make sure we have something for their tummies. They will overindulge." She walked over to one of the cabinets, fretting.

Dominic stood up and slowly bowed. "Thank you for coming, ladies. It's a pleasure to meet you all."

"No… thank you." Roxy gave a deep curtsey. She then kicked her leg up, touched her ear and roared with laughter.

"I'm just glad she's got her knickers on," Marianne said, and Frances laughed.

"Not for long, darling." Roxy snorted with laughter.

"I will be back shortly," announced Dominic. "Please, there are refreshments." He pointed to a long table dressed in red and gold filled with cold meats, pâté, sandwiches and drinks. Cakes and other desserts were arranged on a side table, all illuminated by candles. Streamers, balloons and Chinese lanterns festooned the picture rails and ceiling.

Elsie clasped her hands. "I'll be mother." She rushed over.

"Please let me help. Roxy, dear, what would you like?" asked Frances while surveying the vol-au-vents. "They look delish."

Taking Marianne's arm, Roxy danced around the room. The silhouette of the ladies dancing could be seen from the garden.

Frances looked in awe at Roxy's hourglass figure draped in a powder-blue chiffon dress, moving effortlessly across the highly polished parquet floor.

Roxy laughed as Marianne whirled her round the room. Giddy, she did a cha-cha over to the table of goodies. "Come on, loves, we need a couple of drinkies and then we'll be off." She flung her head back laughing.

A man stood in the doorway, his wide shoulders almost filling the space between the door and the frame as he looked over towards Roxy. He moved towards her.

Frances tapped Marianne's shoulder, and Elsie followed their gaze. They all looked in the direction of the man in a black tuxedo. Roxy balanced pineapple and cheese sticks on the side of her plate. She felt a warm stream of air circling around her, and looked up. Her eyes widened seeing the man towering over her.

"May I have this dance?" the man asked, holding out his hand. It enveloped Roxy's small china doll hands.

She passed Frances her plate, which she balanced on top of her book.

"You could have got a whole plate of those sandwiches into her mouth sideways," Marianne said before knocking back a drink. "What's this again?"

Elsie shook her head as she watched the couple dance. "Snowball I think, but I think Roxy has put her spin on it," she replied, looking at the bottle next to it. "Vodka, vermouth and very little else."

Marianne slurped from the glass. "Fill it up again. It has a certain kick to it." They both watched Roxy continue to glide across the dance floor.

"Steel is at it again. You've got to hand it to him," said a small man with an auburn quiff handing Frances a plate of egg and cress sandwiches.

"He is handsome. Is he an actor?" Frances took a bite from a corner of one of the sandwiches.

"Not far off. A circus performer. He's appeared in films," he said proudly. "I'm Bernard, Bert to my friends."

Frances nodded. "Pleased to meet you, Bert." She put her book down on the table.

Bert craned his neck to read the title. "Is it good?"

"It is. It's a mystery. I like reading." She looked at Bert. "What do you like to read?"

He shrugged. "I don't get much chance, but usually the racing pages." He winked at her, and Frances blushed.

Two more men came in, and they took it in turn to spin the ladies around. One of them lean, and the other more filled out with rosy cheeks.

Marianne offered the plate of sandwiches to the men.

"What have we got here?" asked the lean man.

"Fresh crab," she replied.

"My favourite." He bit into it. "And fresh too." The lean man chewed as he talked.

"Cromer crab," Marianne said proudly.

Roxy cha-cha'd across to the table with Steel.

"Ladies, may I introduce Ralph," said Steel. "There's Alf; he owns the garage in town. And Bert, St Francis of Assisi himself with a menagerie of animals." He tapped each of their heads as he towered over them.

"I've only got a smallholding, but have a lucrative deal with the local co-op, so I have a bit put aside." Bert winked at Frances, and then offered her a piece of Battenberg.

Dominic watched as the residents laughed, drank and danced around the room. Steel then got up on a wooden platform and sang in a rich baritone voice.

"This is the best party I've been to in years. And even better with a handsome man." Roxy held up her glass to Steel as he stood centre stage clasping the microphone. "He croons beautifully."

Dominic stood next to Roxy watching Steel sing.

She put her arms around his waist and gave him a squeeze. "I feel as if I've known you for years and years. You're an absolute poppet." She gave him a big kiss and felt a warmth feeling enter her body. She looked into Dominic's eyes, which had changed to a warm hazel colour. "It feels like I've had a hangover for the last twenty years. God, I must have been on a real bender." She looked at Dominic and winked.

"Funny you should say that. I feel as though I've been on a long journey on a shebang across the continent. I feel a bit sore," Marianne said standing opposite.

"Strange you should mention that. I feel as if I've fallen into one of my Jean Plaidy novels. I could have sworn I've been stranded in a turret," Frances said before taking a swig of her drink. "And held against my will."

Roxy winked at Frances and grabbed Steel's hand as he walked towards her. "I want to go to Paris."

Steel spun her around as Roxy screamed. Bert threw streamers at them.

"I must pick up the children. I'm so worried they'll be hungry," Elsie said, scooping up dishes of jelly and trifle and carefully putting them into paper bags. "They do so like trifle." She sighed heavily. "They have been away a long time." She shook her head. "They must have been on a summer holiday. It seems such a long time since I last saw them. They will be very hungry."

"Tickets! They won't let us in!" Roxy waved a strip of buff-coloured tickets above her head. "Your children will be looked after just beautifully, Elsie. And a couple more hours won't matter a jot. Alf, Bert and Ralf, please join Steel."

Bert pulled out a silk white scarf from inside his jacket pocket. "What do you think?" He winked at Roxy.

"A real dish." She gave him a big kiss. "Come, follow me."

Dominic watched as they went out through the French windows and down onto the patio. The jazz music followed as Chinese lanterns sambaed in the warm evening breeze along the balcony.

"This is my night!" Roxy screamed, kicking up her legs before running amongst the trees.

Marianne and Frances grabbed the croquet box and headed for the manicured lawn. A dog shot out from behind the mulberry bush and ran towards Bert, jumping up at him and attempting to lick his face.

"Bobby! There you are!" Bert laughed as he threw a ball.

Steel took Roxy's hand and walked her to the rose garden, the perfume of the flowers filling the night air. He picked a red damask rose and handed it to Roxy. They embraced passionately.

The voices of Alf, Bert, Frances, Marianne, Elsie and Ralph laughed as they played croquet in the distance.

"That's a hit!" Ralph called.

Bobby scooped up the ball and weaved in and out of their legs. "Bert, you're cheating! You have help!" Marianne shouted.

Dominic stood on the steps of the French windows holding his battered leather bag. Silence hung heavily except for the oscillating fan on the desk and the geezer gurgling in the kitchen.

The front door clanked and creaked as it moaned, and then Nesta walked in singing to herself on her way to the kitchen to make herself a cuppa. The water was cold.

"Bastard thing," she said, flicking the switch up and down. She walked down the corridor and peered around the corner into the women's section and looked over at the desk. It was empty except for the oscillating fan. "Dominic! Are you there, hon?" She walked up the stairs calling his name but got no answer. She checked the toilets and the side rooms. "Bloody typical." She went back to the kitchen and lit a cigarette, blowing smoke up to the ceiling as she hummed. The door swung open.

"Oi oi!" Ed shouted. "How's life in the madhouse?"

Nesta poked her head out of the kitchen. "He's gone and not even left a bloody handover note. I'll have him." She continued to puff on her cigarette.

"That's bang out of order. I'd report him. Give us a ciggie, I'm gasping."

She threw Ed the packet. "Help yourself. I'm off to see how the stinking oldies are doing." She put on her headphones and sang along to the music while walking down the corridor.

Nesta walked into the woman's section still singing as she flung open the French windows and went over to the desk to switch off the lamp. She continued to sing to herself on her way over to the cabinet to fetch the medication for the morning rounds. After placing the array of pills on a trolley, she wheeled it over to Frances.

"Hello, Franny. How's you, babe?" She looked at Frances, who lay staring up at the ceiling, her mouth wide open. She touched her arm. It was cold. "Shit!" She breathed heavily as she stepped back and looked across at Elsie, Marianne and Roxanne. All of them were lying motionless, just staring blankly at the ceiling. She screamed running over to each bed and colliding with the trolley in the process, causing it to topple over.

Ed came running and saw her kneeling on the floor crying hysterically. "What…? What?" Nesta pointed over to the women. He ran across and checked their pulses. "Oh shit! Oh God!" He then ran upstairs to the men's section.

Steel lay in the middle of the room face downwards. He was rigid. Ralph, Alf and Bert were all lying motionless, their bodies like marble and looking up at the ceiling with their eyes wide open. Bert had a smile on his face.

"Shit, this is bad! This is so bad!" Ed ran downstairs and called the emergency number. "We have a situation. Oh God. I can't believe this is happening." He was shaking. "Nesta, what was the name of the agency?"

Nesta was uncontrollably crying. She put her hand to her head. "Guardian Personnel, I think."

Ed checked on his phone. "I can't find the sodding number for them." Then he phoned directory enquiries.

"Guardian Personnel? We cannot find any such number. Are you sure you have the correct name, Caller?"

Ed looked at Nesta. "Check again. You must be wrong. Check now!"

Suddenly, there was a bang on the door. Nesta looked at Ed.

"Here." He passed her the phone. "Check a different spelling. We'll have to call Fiona – she must have details." He ran to the door and pulled it open. Two police officers were standing on the doorstep.

"Good morning. Are you the manager?"

Ed shook his head and trembled. "S-She'll be here shortly."

One of the officers moved forward. "We've received reports about a disturbance early this morning. A lot of screaming coming from the premises."

The other police officer nodded as he read from a printout: "Yes, a number of complaints about a party in the garden last night." He looked up and smiled. "We have to follow these things up. It shouldn't take too long."

Ed stood back as the two police officers walked across the threshold.

"We get a lot of calls about safeguarding." One of the officers smiled at Ed. "I expect it was a birthday party for one of the old dears. Don't worry. We'll be quiet as church mice while we have a look around. I expect they'll be sleeping it off." He laughed as he walked down the hallway.

Breakdown

The countryside is such a beautiful place with its patchwork fields and the omnipotent birdsong, each one carrying a message. If only humans could understand what they are singing.

A thrush sits on a branch chirping, "How are you?"

Or the blackbird announcing, "Rain is on its way." A wren whistles, "There's a real feast at Farmer Harrows'."

Or the crow sitting with its neck arched telling you to, "Beware, there's danger up ahead, turn back now!"

And then there are the trees, those magnificent sentinels of time, many of whom have stood for hundreds of years watching what goes on and witnessing many events, each one transmitting a message to the other. If only we could hear. What would they be telling us?

But, of course, we send messages to the countryside too. We tell it that we'll be developing it for the good of humankind, as it watches powerlessly while officials mark out trees to be slayed and meadows to be euthanised by thousands of tonnes of concrete. And where the intricate patchwork of pastures and trees once stood, housing developments now blossom. Kerbs lowered and vegetation smothered to make way for larger drives to accommodate the gas-guzzling leviathan of the human people carrier. Grass, trees and plants are obsolete as developers go large on each residence but reduce the gardens to pocket size, hemming in each household, causing the occupants to struggle to breathe as they suffer stress, anxiety and depression, and then have to seek help from a GP, who'll eagerly prescribe pills for them to continue scrambling up Maslow's pyramid. The humans are precious over their land, so they go green by installing solar panels, using renewable energy and recycle to reduce their carbon footprint.

But you cannot match that feeling of escaping into the countryside, driving along those narrow lanes on hot summer days, the sunroof open, listening to your favourite songs as you cruise under canopies of trees, shards of light bouncing off the window screen while you catch glimpses of the wildlife. The rabbits foraging for food and, the deep russet brown of a fox breaking cover to move stealthily amongst the foliage. The woman driving her high-performance car, weaving along the country lanes. The birds circling overhead. "What a looker!".

The trees send the message, "Nice car and respectful of the speed limit, too," as they gently sway in time with the music, allowing the light to stream through their branches.

Abby was quite safe in her bubble of technology. The airbags, side impact bars, central locking and seat belts kept her cossetted from the dangers of the city. But it's safe in the countryside. The satnav ensured she drove along the most economical route, which reduced her emissions and thus saved the planet. She tapped her fingers on the leather steering wheel as she accelerated, singing along to the music.

It's been four long years since her husband left, but she'd turned a corner. Her body was the best it had looked in years. She'd engaged the services of a personal trainer and ate well – only organic food touched her lips. A friend helped her to escape her cocoon, and she ventured into internet dating. With the aid of a glass of wine, she scrolled through the profiles, viewing each specimen. *It was merely out of curiosity*, she'd messaged Brad.

They'd spoken a couple of times, including guided virtual tours of each other's houses, and agreed to meet halfway. He was on a much higher salary and lived in a new development with bifolding doors stretching the whole length of the bottom floor.

As she drove, she rehearsed how the evening would go; in her mind's eye it would be perfect. The only interruption was the announcement of the satnav telling her to take the next right ahead. The road was free from traffic and smooth as she cruised along in the countryside heading to a bistro pub, The Green Man. "The colour matches my eyes," she'd jested to Brad in one of their many telephone conversations. She had the most beautiful emerald green eyes, but equally important were the rave reviews of the pub. Ratings were important to her.

The signature dish on the menu was the locally caught trout with green salad – low calorie, so she'd already chosen her meal. She wanted to make a good impression and not appear too excessive. She gently tapped her fingers on the steering wheel and smiled. It was going to be a good evening.

She'd been working on her manifestations as recommended by her therapist to set the direction of her life. Yes, a new man and a new adventure – that's what she'd manifested every night before going to bed. And his bifolding doors leading out onto a large patio made of Portland stone and down to a lounge pool set against a backdrop of the countryside – she'd visualised herself each evening looking out from there with her new man. Yes, life was good, and she felt that Brad was the one.

How dating had changed since she'd first met Alan all those years ago in a pub. Dating was now much simpler. She could shop around in the comfort of her own home browsing the dating apps. It was fun, and she could create her own fantasy. If physical appearance and profession were important, she filtered these with a touch of a button. She always preferred something a little bit different. Natural cotton always creased, but perhaps a bit of nylon wouldn't go amiss. Synthetic helped in appearance. She smiled. The crow's feet were smoother, almost invisible as she looked at herself in her rear-view mirror. Yes, the apps were a godsend. She was busy, but she could fit in browsing time.

Each night she added more filters: solvent, must be over six feet tall – ideally over six feet, four inches – good complexion, hobbies and, yes, nice teeth. She smiled again – the veneers looked good.

The sun streamed through her hair, her roots had been touched up last weekend, and she looked sun-kissed with her tan. In her manifestations, she was walking with her partner in the Maldives, or San Marino, no, Sorrento, or along the canal in Venice, or they'd go on a cruise. She liked the water, but the countryside was far more romantic. Walking in a meadow hand in hand or lying side by side listening to the beautiful chorus of the evening birdsong. This was going to be a wonderful evening.

She loved her automatic car; it made driving along the lanes so easy. The satnav announced that she needed to take the second left. It was only another five miles. She decreased her speed to enjoy the early evening and the scenery. A deer then strolled out ahead and looked at her. She slowed down and smiled, allowing the creature to cross. She took a deep breath and exhaled slowly. Yes, it was wonderful being out in the countryside.

Her thoughts shifted back to Brad. He'd mentioned that he was a director with a housing developer. "I was originally a town planner, but luck came knocking," he'd said, smiling.

Abby had had a lucky break, too. "I was in advertising, more office support, and a manager was off sick, so I stepped into her shoes. And now I run my own department, manage over a hundred staff and travel to other offices. I have a healthy portfolio."

They were well matched. The glass was definitely half full.

"Do you like snorkelling?" he'd asked. She'd only done it once off the Great Barrier Reef.

"I love it," she'd cooed. Afterwards, she'd looked for a local snorkelling group and booked in a few lessons. That's the beauty of technology – you could see what's around immediately. She assured herself, he won't know; what he doesn't know won't hurt. And besides, imitation is the sincerest form of flattery.

A friend had giggled, saying, "Oh, I envy your glamour. It's so good to be single and attract such a stunning-looking guy like Brad." Her friend sighed. "And you, Abby, are stunning. Those eyes – who wouldn't be attracted to them?"

Life was good for Abby. She'd moved to a newer development last year after selling her previous house for a healthy profit from the proceeds of a fat divorce settlement. "Buy cheap, buy twice," her mother would often quote when younger. So she engaged the best lawyer she could afford.

Adultery came with a hefty price tag, and one which Abby would ensure yielded her a healthy return. There was over £200,000 spare for perhaps somewhere in the country. Yes, she would like that. She could do it up at weekends even though it would take time.

"Wow, I'm about to look out for a project too. I was thinking the Cotswolds. I just love the countryside." Brad smiled upon hearing the news. They had so much in common.

She continued singing along and tapped her fingers in time. The satnav informed her to take the next right; it was only another four miles. A message pinged from Brad: *ETA 5 mins. See you shortly ttfn xx*. She smiled and lifted her foot off the accelerator. She had elevated calves which looked good in her black patent shoes. She kept her legs toned by always keeping them slightly raised as she drove. She didn't need to hurry.

Abby flicked a switch which opened the sunroof some more, allowing the air to circulate. The country air was much nicer than air con and purer than the stuffiness of the city. The car glided along as she sang and laughed to herself at the conversations she'd had with Brad. He had a good sense of humour. How he made her laugh. She'd not laughed so hard in years.

Just then, the satnav beeped announcing a diversion. There had been an accident up ahead. She looked at the display and tapped the screen for more information. A map popped up indicating where the diversion would take her and the time estimate. It would take another ten minutes. She still had time and continued driving.

Lights in the rear-view mirror dazzled her; making her wince. It was a car tailgating her. As she accelerated, a bird dive-bombed towards the windscreen, causing her to swerve. Technology helped to correct her handling of the car, but the tailgater was now flashing their headlights. The road was too narrow to pull over. She accelerated more, but the car behind also increased its speed. Abby looked at the satnav, which alerted her to the new route. She had to take the next left. It would take her through a number of villages including Braydene, a mediaeval hamlet. The driver continued flashing their lights.

Panic swirled up inside her, so she accelerated more as thoughts flashed through her mind whether she could pull in tight to the verge just to let the maniac past. Then her thoughts raced frantically about the driver being a serial killer – she'd heard about such things. She accelerated more.

An alarm sounded and a light flashed on her dashboard warning of her speed. The car behind was now going even faster. It reared up behind, virtually touching her bumper while continuing to flash and sound the horn. She could feel her neck and face getting hot; her heart was beating fast. She was hyperventilating. She couldn't breathe and felt dizzy. Things were looking blurry as the car's headlights reflected off the mirror making it difficult for her to see. She was going to crash.

A group of starlings screamed overhead, "Beware!" as the car behind tried to overtake, but a car was coming in the opposite direction, causing it to break hard. She screamed and gripped the steering wheel. Making her jump, the satnav pinged as it announced that the diversion was two miles away.

Perspiration was running down her face, stinging her eyes. She felt hot and clammy as the car continued to intimidate and bully her. Pushing her foot harder against the accelerator, she weaved around the corners. "Come on!" she screamed, feeling the car vibrate.

The car behind disappeared from view and she continued to race around the hairpin bends, the back wheels lifting off the road, alarms and lights flashing on her dashboard. She eased slightly off the accelerator still checking her mirror. The car was nowhere to be seen. Glancing at the satnav, she'd soon be joining the dual carriageway. There would be more traffic. She'd be safe.

Her breathing became less laboured. She eased her foot off the accelerator and her thoughts drifted back to Brad as she looked at the time. She was nearly there, so she relaxed while driving under a canopy of trees, the light cutting through the branches and onto the silhouette of a kestrel flying majestically overhead. Just for a moment she was lost in its beauty, the bird gently gliding in mid-air, its body contrasting against the blue sky. It began to circle, funnelling slowly downwards. Within a split second, its speed quickened as it fluttered its wings and without warning dived down onto its prey.

Then, Abby screamed. Her car was shunted forwards. The car was back behind her roaring and about to hit her again. She slammed her foot down hard on the accelerator. The satnav pinged announcing that the dual carriageway was not far away now, but the car behind lunged forward, hitting her again. Screaming, she swerved and turned down a narrow lane, clipping the side of the verge while zigzagging and pressing her foot down further on the accelerator. The driver behind slammed on the brakes and reversed, pausing momentarily, watching Abby while she continued driving down the long, dark, narrow lane, and then it drove off.

The sun disappeared behind a row of cypress trees and the air grew cooler. Abby closed the sunroof and then looked at the satnav recalculating as she continued checking her mirror. The car was not following her. The lane began to narrow even more, and the smoothness gave way to shingle and a dirt track. She pulled over and looked at her phone. There was no signal and the satnav was still recalculating. The lane was too narrow to turn. She'd have to reverse and head back up to the main road.

Once she put the car into reverse, it steadily moved backwards, but her foot slipped and hit the accelerator, causing the car to lurch forward and hit a tree stump. A warning sounded and a light came on telling her that the back tyre had low pressure. She could now hear a hissing sound.

Under normal circumstances she'd change the tyre, but she was wearing a white calico dress cut slightly above the knee, which would be ruined. She'd call for a recovery vehicle if she had a signal. How annoying she hadn't manifested this happening.

Abby took her cardigan from the backseat and slipped it on before heading back up the road to see if she could get a signal and call Brad. He'd pick her up. She remembered that he'd described himself as a "gallant knight in shining armour". Yes, he would come and fetch her.

It was five-thirty. Brad had last texted fifteen minutes ago. They were due to meet now. It was a woman's prerogative to be late. She'd got out of worse situations than this, and they'd had lengthy conversations about each other's core values.

"Trust is important. Without it, what are you left with?" Brad had quoted when he signed off each time from their telephone calls. *Brad will understand.* She continued to walk up the dark, narrow lane.

It was becoming overcast and the temperature had dropped. Abby pulled the cardigan closer around her body as she walked under the branches of an elm where a thrush sang. She looked up at the dark, ominous clouds stirring overhead. She turned to go back to the car for an umbrella. *No, I need to get a signal and call Brad.*

There were trees up ahead – they would provide sufficient cover if the heavens opened. The thrush's singing grew louder urging, "Dear lady, there is rain, go back to your car." The skies darkened, and Abby could feel specks of rain. There was a cedar tree ahead that would offer her protection, or should she go back to the car? *No, I'll head for the trees to get a signal.*

The spots were gathering momentum, so she broke into a gallop heading for shelter, the rain now pelting down. The thick branches of the cedar tree shielded her from the wet. It gently swayed in the breeze. "Please, my dear, return to your car," it warned. She checked her phone, but there was still no signal. As she stood with her arms folded and shivering, a pheasant poked out from under the hedgerow. It shook its head.

"You fool" and then disappeared.

Abby stepped out from under the tree looking around and saw a field. *I'll get a signal there.* She looked at the low drystone wall and figured it wouldn't be too hard to climb it. She was fit and agile and would wait until the last dark cloud had drifted away. She looked at the sky. It was strange because no rain was forecast. Looking at her watch, it was five-forty. Her heart quickened. *I'm still in the safe zone, but for how long?* Oh, how she wished she'd texted Brad to tell him there was a diversion and that she might be late. But surely Brad would understand?

A bond had developed over the weeks. All their conversations and everything they had in common. Brad would understand. He'd pick her up, and they would have that nice evening together while her car was being looked at. Perhaps this was fate and they would spend the night together. Yes, it was going to work out well.

Looking up once more, she noticed that the clouds were getting darker overhead and the rain continued. She found a ledge and leant against it. The lichen was dry so would easily wipe off.

A wren flew down, sat on a branch above her and chirped. She watched as it moved its head to one side looking down at her. "You're a pretty boy." She smiled while it continued to sing. "I hope you're like Brad. Have you come to see if I'm okay? You couldn't get me a signal, could you?" The wren flew away. She watched it going from one tree to another. Each tree bowed slightly as if in conversation. Abby closed her eyes and visualised a manifestation: a phone signal and Brad arriving smiling. Yes, she could see it now. Brad arriving in his long, sleek car and carrying her into the passenger seat and making a fuss of her. Of course, she'd manifest that the rain would stop first.

The rain eased, the sun breaking through the clouds. Abby clasped her hands looking up to the sky. "Thank you." She made her way along the drystone wall, holding her phone above her head to catch a passing signal. As she approached a bend in the wall, she heard a beeping sound. "Yes, thank you!" She opened her texts. *I'm here, what drink would you like? Champagne cocktail looks good?* She smiled reading Brad's text. She was about to call him, but her phone pinged and another six messages came through.

The second was a text from her mother about whether she could pick up her dry cleaning. Another from work asking her to call because there was a problem. She'd leave that until later. She attempted to call Brad, but another text pinged. She read it: *Are you okay?* It was followed by other texts: *Where are you?* And then another: *It's 6pm. I'm off in 10 mins.* And a final text message: *???* His texts had been sent in five-minute bursts.

Abby rang his number, but it went straight to voicemail. She was about to leave a message when the phoned beeped announcing that it was out of reception. She screamed, "Why me?" Her echoes carried down the lane as a crow gave a raspy caw in her direction. It was now 6:10 p.m. Abby ran up the lane. She had to speak to Brad.

"I'm the patient sort of guy." She could hear him laughing. They'd laugh about this in weeks to come. "Do you remember me breaking down and you thought I'd stood you up," she'd say. They'd both find it hilarious, sitting there in the lounge pool drinking champagne. Yes, Brad would understand; they had so much in common.

Stretching her arm upwards as though flying a kite, she hoped to catch a signal. But nothing. She ran faster, and then stumbled as the heel broke off her shoe.

A crow looked down craning its neck. "Go back. Go back now," he squawked. And then there was a loud beeping sound.

"A signal!" she cried. Her hands shook calling Brad. It went straight to voicemail again. "Brad, it's Abby. Look, I've…" The phone pinged to announce no signal. She screamed.

A sparrow nearby tweeted, "I'm sorry."

Her aberration lasted a couple of moments, and then she ran over to the wall and leant against it. Catching her reflection in her phone screen, her mascara had run and her lipstick was smeared. Brad would surely understand. People are late for legitimate reasons. "I'm very gallant," she heard his voice echo. He'd understand. She cried frantically waving the phone above her head.

The dark clouds drifted slowly across as the sun broke through and a warmth radiated down. Abby removed her cardigan. That was the beauty of the countryside: it returns to the status quo very quickly and the sun makes everything look better. Brad would call apologising and pick her up. She'd fall into his arms. *"Yes, soppy, but what the hell?"* She laughed out loud.

A large bird hopped awkwardly onto the drystone wall. Its plumage pulled back as it lifted its head and screeched, startling Abby. It drew up its feathers exposing the beautiful colours. Yes, a peacock is such an elegant bird; but its call, why does it sound like a woman screaming? Its screech echoed down the lane and across the field. Its presence had awakened the countryside and, in the distance, a dark figure could be seen in the middle of the field.

It was a scarecrow strapped to a long pole. It moved slightly in the breeze. It was old and made of many throwaway items. There was straw from previous harvests and branches from trees felled from the highways because they were deemed too dangerous for passing motorists. It had a hat from the farmer's grandfather and the eyes, they were dark and hollow – soulless. Rarely did it stir, but today it gently swayed on its post, creaking in the summer breeze.

Suddenly, it swung around in the direction of Abby. Crows sat in the branches watching. A tree leant to one side. The scarecrow's face appeared to move. Perhaps it was the breeze or was it a twitch? But no, its head rose slowly upwards as though trying to breathe. It had awoken, stirred from his slumbers.

"It wasn't me," tweeted the robin.

"Nor me," the wren chirped back in return.

The peacock looked up and said, "I did try to warn her."

A rabbit looked across saying, "I'll warn her." It ran over to Abby, darting about, and sat looking up at her. She smiled as it slammed its back foot loudly onto the ground. It repeated it again and again, but Abby was lost in thought thinking of Brad. "I tried!" the rabbit cried before dashing into a bush.

The scarecrow looked across, its hollow eyes watching Abby walk along the lane.

"Please don't," the wren begged. "She's lost. She'll be gone soon, I promise."

The scarecrow sniffed the air, its head moving in Abby's direction. It was too late.

Abby continued walking along singing to herself; she found this helped her when feeling anxious. Brad would pick her up. She continued to wave the phone above her head trying to catch a signal.

"What a lot of fuss," her mother would say when Abby got upset. "There now, hush your noise and think of happy thoughts." Her mother was good at making things appear better. Abby smiled thinking of a lovely evening sitting in the beer garden. "No news is good news," she heard her mother's voice repeat.

The main road wasn't far. Hopefully, even for a nanosecond, she could text her location. Brad would know she'd broken down. "I'd say I have considerable emotional intelligence," Abby recalled him mentioning in one of their earlier telephone conversations. But then she stopped – she could hear something.

A lark overhead sang, "Run for your life!"

It was the sound of traffic. Yes, a car. She smiled. It was Brad. Yes, he'd found her.

She quickened her pace and broke into a canter. A rustling in the field matched her speed. She could see Brad. Yes, Brad would be waiting at the top of the road. But she reduced her speed as reality hit her.

"You idiot! How would he know?" She slowed down and then screamed as a searing pain shot through her foot. She limped over to the drystone wall crying with blood oozing from her. There was a piece of glass wedged in the side of her foot. A piece of a broken bottle left by humans on their visit to the countryside. She needed to remove it. She braced herself and let out another scream when she quickly whipped it out.

Taking a strip from the lining of her dress to stem the blood flow, she pressed her hand hard against the wound and sat on the wall crying. "Where are you, Brad?"

A robin sat down beside her and pulled down its wings, exposing its red breast. "Danger! Danger!" it chirped.

Abby swiped her hand. "Leave me alone!" she cried, sitting hunched up on the wall.

The scarecrow licked its lips and slowly released itself from the post. It breathed in deeply and looked at Abby. *Such a nice scent* as it put its head down and ran in her direction, darting from one wheat row to another, its presence only betrayed by the sound of rustling spears.

Abby continued to wipe away her tears with the cuff of her cardigan, and then looked around when she heard a sound coming from across the field. She could see a ripple effect of the wheat crop bending slightly forward and fanning towards her. The outline grew more intense as the pattern changed rapidly moving closer to her.

She stood up and smiled. "A dog." She laughed. "Come here, boy!" she shouted, waving her arms. *Its owner can't be far behind.* "Good boy!" she cried. *Yes, it's a dog. And the owner.* She looked out towards the field. *A farmer will be somewhere, and he'll help.*

She hobbled forwards wincing in pain and calling out. The wheat spears yielded as the pattern grew closer and louder while being pummelled hard by the scarecrow's fists. Abby moved her arms up and down hysterically. She wanted a hot bath and to go to bed. She'd call Brad tomorrow after a good night's sleep. Yes, a good night's sleep would help.

"It will all come out in the wash," her mother often said as Abby stood awaiting the presence of her rescuer.

"Over here!" she called, signalling with her arms.

A thrush swooped down, narrowly missing the scarecrow's head as it charged towards her. Abby had decided to sit on the wall and swing her legs around so they would be dangling in the field. Starlings descended on the tree above screeching down. She put her hands to her ears. "Please stop! I can't bear the sound anymore!" she cried, closing her eyes tight. She didn't like lots of noise and began talking to herself, "It will be all right. Just count to ten."

She counted slower, and then opened her eyes at ten. Everywhere around was quiet. She looked up to see that there were no birds. Everywhere was totally still. She looked out across the field, but nothing was moving. There was no dog yapping at her heels. Where had the dog gone? She called out, "Here, boy!" She looked down at her phone and saw one small bar appearing. "Thank you!" she cried and quickly dialled. No, she'd text Brad and then call. He'd pick up the texts first. *Broken down... Sorry... Hurt myself... I'm...* she looked around *...about ten mins from the pub.* Yes, Abby was sure that she wasn't far as she finished texting.

The scarecrow perched on the wall watching her, paused for a moment and craned its head to one side looking at her delicate hands caress the keys. She was so graceful. It pulled up its head and smelt the air. Her scent was so sweet. Abby dialled a number and listened waiting for the phone to connect. She felt so tired. *I want to sleep for a week.* She closed her eyes and sat manifesting her dreams while the phone continued to ring. Brad would be running her a bath and she would be there drinking a cocktail and enjoying the bubbles around her tired, aching limbs.

She rested her head to one side as she drifted deeper. The scarecrow slowly moved along, causing a dislodged stone to fall to the ground. Abby stirred, but soon closed her eyes again.

"Where is the dog?" she murmured. "Here, boy."

The scarecrow crawled along the wall licking its lips. Abby could feel a shadow. She smiled. "Good boy." The owner was probably with him. She shivered feeling a shadow loom over her. She opened her eyes and stared into two deep hollows.

The countryside is a wonderful place. The rolling hedgerow and patchwork of fields so inviting to the stressed city types as they escape the urban jungle to relax.

"I love the countryside." A woman looked up. "Brad, can we pull over there and walk along the field. It looks wonderful."

He smiled. "As I said before, I'm gallant. It's so nice to meet someone with the same values and interests." He moved his hand along her arm before turning off the main road and down a long, dark, narrow lane and pulling over.

The woman got out and swung her arms around. "This is wonderful. Come on, I'll race you." She pulled herself onto the top of the drystone wall and jumped into the field. Brad vaulted over after her. "Show off." She laughed. "I'll race you to the scarecrow." Screaming as Brad gave chase, she kicked off her shoes and ran.

Brad stood watching her as she turned waving. How he loved her beautiful bee-stung lips which everyone commented on.

The summer breeze stirred. The scarecrow moved gently on its post and slowly opened its emerald green eyes.

Restitution

Have you ever wondered when sitting somewhere, perhaps in a park, on a bus, train or in a café, whether you have a connection with someone next to you? When I mean connection, have your paths crossed before? Perhaps through a mutual friend or indirectly by the process of having something once in your possession, money from a cashpoint, a pair of jeans you tried on but discarded because they didn't fit or something else? Or whether they've committed a crime or are contemplating doing so. Would I or anyone else be able to sense it?

Things like this often go through my mind. I even think about how many would be the victims of murder, or whether they're plotting to murder someone. And what would happen if you could read their thoughts? Or worse, they could read yours? My friends tell me that I think too much and I have an unhealthy mind to think about such dark things. I don't see anything wrong with how I think.

As I sat pondering on the bus on the way to work, I remembered an article I read some time ago claiming we can each tap into each other's thoughts. It went into detail about the neural pathways of the brain and that neurons mirror those that are in close proximity which can develop over time. It used the example of a mobile phone system and that all calls, messages and downloads each use preset channels, and just maybe you tuned into the same channel as someone else and can download or access their thoughts and memories. Maybe I could send a message to the people walking by. What message would I send? And what would happen if they could hear the message? Would they help me or refer it to someone else?

A few days later, I was sitting in the park – something I do often – and a young guy walked by deep in conversation on his phone laughing and smiling. You know the situation, you think they're talking to you but they're wearing earphones. I closed my eyes and focused my attention and directed it towards him. I repeated the thought over and over again, opened my eyes and watched him. He stopped, turned, looked at me and stared. He was attractive, not quite a business type, more local government or perhaps IT. Yes… he had an "IT look" about him. You know the person, hair sticking up one side, perhaps gaming all night, and his shoes unpolished with worn-down heels. His trousers had two deep creases as a result of being hung incorrectly. You could see the telltale stains under the armpits – the white marks you get with a build-up of cheap deodorants.

I think my gaze lingered too much, and our eyes locked into a stare. I felt embarrassed. I didn't want to appear rude, so pretended to recognise something as I flashed a smile across my face. I hope he didn't think I was smiling at him. It was strange, he turned his head, a double take as they call it, as he walked by the café which sells instant coffee, stewed tea from an antiquated tea urn and polystyrene sandwiches. I'm surprised it's still in business, but there you go, some things don't change. He did it a third time. Yes… he just flipped his head around a third time. It was more longing this time. I wondered if he'd felt someone staring at him. Or perhaps he thought I knew something about him. Maybe he was having a secret assignation. Yes… that was it, an assignation with a married woman, someone much older, or a man. I hear there are a lot of men who "cottage", at least that's the term they use. I laughed when I first heard this expression. It conjured up images of nice old dears having tea and cakes in some quaint setting, not some sordid place where men buggered each other. Or maybe he'd picked up the message I had transmitted.

The new manager started today. She's tall, Welsh, seems nice enough and has a habit of putting "then" at the end of sentences. Are you okay, then? Where does this go, then?

In her introduction, she announced changes to the company processes – she's big on processes. We gathered in the media room and she went through a slide presentation. For some reason there was an IT hitch and she ended up using the white board. She talked fast and stumbled over her words. When she looked at us, we strained to understand as her pace quickened. She bleated several set phrases. "We'll all have to ensure we're singing from the same hymn sheet." She drew circles on the board and pointed arrows. "We need to think more outside the box. Moving forward, we need more things on the dashboard, and I'll be working out a matrix to create a greater resilience to avoid being kicked into the long grass." She put the pen down looking pleased with herself. "Any questions?" She looked at the sea of faces. "If we can get into groups, I'll hand out some flash cards," she announced.

The card she placed in front of me said, "What can you bring to the table?"

Tara nudged me and whispered, "A casserole."

Nula, that's the new manager's name, went around each table asking for answers and shared them with the group. She wrote them on the board and circled particular ones and how these could be incorporated into the core values.

As the session ended, Nula attempted to wipe the pen off the board, but after a few moments realised she'd used an indelible marker. "What a bloody stupid thing to do. Who is responsible for facilities?" She looked around the room.

Nula wanted a clean slate. At first I thought she said she was introducing slate, and then imagined a truck load of Blaenau Ffestiniog slate arriving at the office. No, she meant she wanted to "reset" and would be carrying out appraisals. It was all a bit odd, as she didn't know us. She would be doing them alphabetically and as my surname was Adams, I would be one of the first.

She introduced a new appraisal system, similar to what we had at school, and I was marked C minus. While she said I was "personable" – yes… that is the word she used, personable – she thought the way I worked was messy – "erratic" she called it – and offered some changes before handing me a list.

I looked down at it. She had come up with ten separate processes in place of the previous four. I scratched my head as I looked at the diagram, turning it one way and then another, but I still couldn't work out where it began or finished. The whole process was a little bit odd and our conversation, if you can call it that, was more of a monologue.

"You'll need to embrace our core values and ensure you make a difference every day." She smiled. Her face lit up the more she criticised.

Towards the end, she seemed to pity me; and as she talked in her staccato Welsh accent, I couldn't help but notice the colour of her face. Orange. She had a tidemark around her neck where the orange met her pasty flesh. It reminded me of the dark rim you get when you've not cleaned the bath for ages. I smiled back, but I was dying inside – dying to walk out, to say something. It was no good. I couldn't get angry. I am not made that way. I had been here for over twenty years, and this was the first time I'd been told I was useless.

"Well, I expect you have lots to do. I'm chocka." Her phone went off. "Hiya, cariad. Yes…" She passed me the form while continuing to talk. "Never, I'm bursting." She laughed hysterically as she ushered me out.

The traffic was heavy. I sat at the traffic lights with Nula's conversation whirling around my head. I didn't see the lights change and someone beeped me. I stalled. The driver behind repeatedly sounded his horn. When I got back to my flat, I continued to mull over the day's events, analysing every word she'd said, replaying the conversations ad nauseum. I climbed into bed exhausted and pulled the covers over. I woke up at 2 a.m. and turned over, but the list of suggested improvements and the sound of her voice consumed my mind.

Nula had been with us for three months, and she'd changed the office colour scheme twice. Gone were the muted tones, in were vibrant red and orange, which were then downgraded to yellow and lilac. Desks were hemmed in together, and stationery was centralised and monitored. Anything out of place would result in an email.

The weekly electronic newsletter had a big picture of Nula announcing the weekly round-up and what she would be doing over the weekend and pictures of her in running gear with a huge Welsh flag across her chest. The following week there was a picture of Nula and the slogan "Welcome to the Board" – she had been promoted to the board of directors. Her meteoric rise was unheard of, and she was quoted as being a "breath of fresh air" who would be moving the company forward. "Over a cliff," someone hissed from the desk two rows in front.

A new desk rota had been introduced as hot-desking was going to be the norm. For some reason, I was seated next to the double doors which led to the service lift. It was a lot darker, so I smuggled in a lamp which I could clamp to the side of the desk. I hoped I'd get used to the door banging against my chair and the draught. I decided to wear a jumper.

Tara raised the new desks in one of the catch-up meetings.

Nula stared, asking, "Is there a problem? Perhaps you've outgrown the organisation." This was her stock answer to anyone who questioned or challenged Nula, as she only liked solutions not problems. She always responded with a wide smile, which often meant a referral to your line manager for a "catch-up". Everyone left the meetings quietly each week.

At lunchtimes, when the weather was good, I'd rush out, head for the park and find somewhere to sit and eat my sandwiches and just people-watch. I'd see the regulars. The office joggers doing a circuit. You could tell the new additions as they straggled, pitching forward catching their breath. One puffed on an inhaler. Young mothers walked around in pairs. "We've had underfloor heating," I overheard one woman proudly announce. Her friend gushed over the news. My seat was like that of the auditorium in a theatre watching the show unfold and when I saw "Mr Brown Shoes", the guy I'd seen the other day who I thought worked in IT, he looked relaxed, surprisingly more well-kempt as his shirt was tucked in and his trousers were less creased. Maybe he'd found love. He was smiling and more attentive. I sat watching while eating my sandwiches. It was Tuesday, so it was cheese and tomato. I also had a hot drink from my aluminium flask.

I noticed with interest – somebody new had entered the park. He was walking along with a newspaper under his arm. Tall with a fitted grey-bluish suit. It was good quality and I thought it would have looked good on me if I'd been taller. He didn't fit into this setting. I watched as he walked up the steps to the small veranda which surrounded the park café; he paused and looked around. I felt embarrassed for him. It's strange how we're so conscious of how we look to each other.

I continued to watch. He must have arranged to meet someone, but who? It's not the sort of café you would go out of your way for. It's difficult to find for a start and the racing green colour blends into the flora of the surroundings.

He bought a sandwich. Probably a salad one to be on the safe side. You just don't know when the café prepares them. I can't imagine they have more than one star for their food rating. He found a seat at the front and had a newspaper, a broadsheet too, and no phone. I saw him as a city type. He turned one of the pages and then looked at his watch. He was shuffling his weight in the chair and then looked up, but a group of school children walked past blocking my view. They were screaming with their heads and arms bobbing up and down like a shoal of salmon swimming upstream – enough to give you seasickness. A couple of adults yelled, but the kids continued screaming and one threw a stone and ran off wailing. He was leaving. I stood up to get a better view. Who was he meeting? All I could see was a dark silhouette of a figure. I couldn't tell if it was a man or a woman.

Later that week, I was given a verbal warning. Nula had carried out a desk inspection. Mine had breached her new policy of everything being cleared away by 5:30 p.m. She took photographs on her phone and sent them to HR. I was surprised she had the time given she claimed she was always "chocka". I had a note on my desk scribbled in black marker. I imagined her perfectly manicured red nails as she signed her name and underlined it twice with two thick lines and an explanation mark. I was on her radar.

    I met up with Charles for lunch. I neglected to mention the warning as I didn't want it to dominate the conversation. I wanted to steer it more to how things were going with him. He worked in the accounts department. We'd started at the same time and had been in the same company induction and shared similar views, so we'd stayed in touch. We met up every few weeks for lunch and sometimes after work for a drink. Our conversation often drifted and we both sat people-watching. Charles was excellent at giving a running commentary using different voices.

"There we have Von Hess doing a dead letter drop for Agent 'X'," he said in a Germanic voice. "He needs to assassinate someone very important." He looked at me.

"Nula," we both said in unison.

We always had a really good belly laugh and agreed to meet up in a couple of weeks, but before leaving I saw Mr Brown Shoes, he looked distant, something was playing on his mind. Charles suggested he was doing county lines supplying to the city types. I watched the man in the grey-bluish suit again. Perhaps Charles was right.

Work became relentless as Nula brought in more changes and decided to buy snack machines for the kitchen which she'd expanded. "I'm thinking of you all," she declared as she stood unveiling them. "Look at this beautiful space I've created. You can have your lunch near to your desks." That was Nula's ploy. She didn't want you to be far away for her to bark orders. She also brought in a new purchase-ordering system, which created more problems than it solved.

One of the section heads, Theo, protested, "The team is working flat out. The new system has caused the delays. We need more resources."

Nula stood up, walked over to him and hovered. "Thank you for sharing that, cariad, but what do you suggest?"

Theo listed the problems as Nula's personal assistant frantically scribbled them down. When he'd finished, there was a deathly silence. Nula took the list and marched into her office, her personal assistant trailing behind her.

Three weeks later I heard that Theo had been dismissed. He'd been with the firm for over seventeen years. I hadn't seen him for a couple of weeks and had assumed he was on annual leave. I remembered seeing him a few days after the incident sitting on a park bench looking out across the lake. I wanted to go up to him, but felt I would have been intruding. I sensed he needed to be alone. I wish I'd reached out to him. What would he do now? His wife was disabled after a car accident, and I'd heard that Nula didn't give references, not even a tombstone one. I tried calling him, but he never answered.

Tara organised a collection away from the prying eyes of Nula's personal assistant and arranged flowers for Theo's wife, a couple of bottles of wine and vouchers for the garden centre. "He looked in good spirits, as though a weight had been lifted off his mind," Tara told me over lunch in the park.

Friday was always a busy day, as all the departments would play catch-up and email urgent invoices and purchase orders that had to be paid by 5 p.m. It was the same every Friday, so we coined it "Jazz Hands Friday". Tara and a couple of others waved our hands as we wobbled our voices, but none of us could emulate Nula's. Her contralto voice, which could easily descale a kettle, travelled throughout the office. You could hear her organising various lunch dates and snorting with laughter.

"Oh don't, I am bursting," she would repeat. "He's awful bard. He put his back out playing. He's been bothering with the boys again." We knew all about her husband Luke's role at the local rugby club and his job as site supervisor with one of the large building firms. He was doing so well. "He's virtually running it single-handedly." She had photographs of Luke dotted around her office standing proudly in his rugby top with his beer gut spilling over his shorts.

Nula came into the office each day at eleven announcing how she'd worked through the night. She'd be out for lunch just before one-thirty and rarely stayed beyond five.

"I'll work from home," she would announce, her perfume wafting past as she dragged a suitcase on wheels. "I'll ping you an email later, cariad, if I'm not too buggered up." She talked loudly into her mobile while walking through the office. "It's manic. I've had two hundred emails today, cariad." Nula provided a daily commentary about the number of emails she'd received, which were then redistributed to us throughout the day.

"That woman would delegate flushing the toilet!" Tara snapped when she opened one of these emails. We both watched as Nula disappeared into the lift snorting with laughter. Tara mouthed something and looked across at me. I smiled.

Four weeks later I headed for the park and saw Charles sitting at one of the picnic benches. He beckoned me over. He was shaking.

"Have you seen it?" He passed me his phone.

"I can't see."

He enlarged the font so I could read the headline "Local Man Found Hanged". The articled detailed how Theo Rathbourne had been unwell with depression. The toll of looking after his invalid wife and being dismissed from his job after seventeen years had culminated in him being found hanging in the master bedroom of his three-bed semi-detached house. I felt so guilty. I should have spoken to him. Both Charles and I looked at each other. Theo had been with the company for years, and he was simply rubbed out because he spoke the truth.

Theo's funeral wouldn't be for several weeks as the coroner's office were still carrying out their enquiries. A group of us arranged to go to his funeral. There were no announcements of Theo's death in Nula's "weekly catch-up", just events outlining Nula's achievements and her posing for a picture outside a new crèche.

The only acknowledgement of Theo was a barbed comment Nula made: "He obviously had a lot on his plate, poor dab."

I put in a request for leave to attend Theo's funeral. My request was turned down, but I appealed, and Nula relented; albeit, she would only allow me to have an extended lunch break. "It's business critical because we need all the invoices processing."

Nula left early to attend a business function. She'd nominated herself for an award.

Jenny from the post room was tearful. "I've had a guts full. I'm taking a job closer to home. The money is less but I'll manage."

We talked about things and the fact that she'd been with the firm for over ten years. I put my arm around her, and she began to cry. It was only then she told me that Nula had given her the option of resigning with grace or being put through a disciplinary. "Just think of it as leaving under a cloud. It wouldn't look good, would it, cariad?" Nula had suggested. Jenny recalled how, upon leaving Nula's office, she heard her talking on the phone saying, "That's another piece of dead wood out of this place." Nula had a collection of set phrases she'd use.

One she said to me on more than one occasion was, "Pride before a fall," whenever you gave her news she didn't want to hear.

A week later it was Jenny's leaving do, and I worked through my lunch so I could leave just after five. I was about to head off when Nula's personal assistant asked me to see Nula. She sat on the edge of her desk and had a file next to her. She'd circled a date with red pen. Apparently, I'd booked in the wrong conference. There was a clash with one of her dates, which I should have known. It was a big conference and meant a lot to the company. I remembered checking with her personal assistant, who had confirmed the correct dates, but before I could even protest, Nula stood up.

"I'd watch what you say very carefully. You are a problem – and one I'll be solving." She glared at me. "I'm suspending you with immediate effect. Gather your things and go."

I froze. I could feel my throat closing. I steadied myself just enough to walk out. I hadn't made any mistakes. I walked over to my desk and gathered my things. People around me watched, and two office juniors helped me. I couldn't remember much, although someone hugged me near the lift, but I can't remember who and as I left the building, Bart the security guard held the door open for me. He placed his hand on my shoulder, pressed it gently and whispered something, but I couldn't quite hear what he said. I walked to the carpark. Everywhere I looked I could see people talking, but I couldn't hear anything. And then Mr Brown Shoes came out from a building opposite. As he rushed past, he looked at me, nodded, and then carried on.

Later that evening, I sat staring blankly at the television. I can't even remember what programmes were on as I flicked between channels. The only images I could see were of Nula standing there glaring, and then Theo, hanging from the ceiling, as Nula stood at the bottom tugging the rope, laughing.

I went to bed late and tried to sleep. I couldn't. All I could see was me sleeping in a shop doorway. I remembered seeing a man sitting at the entrance of the park with a cardboard sign. He'd seen active service in Bosnia, his face weather-beaten and ravaged by life, but always managed a smile when I gave him some money for a cup of coffee. I sat on the edge of the bed, looked out of my fifth-floor flat window across the city and into the distance. I could see our office block. It had two red flashing lights attached to the mobile mast.

I was placed on "garden leave". The irony is that the only garden I have is a spider plant on a shelf in the kitchen. I heard the sound of the letter box and something fall onto the mat. I picked up the letter, put it on the table and stared at it, and then I went out to get a paper before I ripped open the envelope and read the opening paragraph.

I must attend a disciplinary hearing and I could face dismissal for gross misconduct.

Charles phoned. He said he would come with me. I refused; I didn't want him to be the next moving target. I thanked him for his offer, but I had to do this alone.

I went for a walk. I didn't know where I was heading. I just walked and found myself in the park next to work. Finding a seat next to the lake, I watched the ripples on the water and then saw a figure in the distance. It was Mr Brown Shoes. He was on his phone laughing. He didn't see me. I watched him stroll past; he wasn't in a hurry. He paused and looked back, smiled and walked on. I returned the gesture and continued to watch the sun go down before walking back home. There was an eerie stillness as I walked back, and I fell into the deepest sleep I'd had in ages.

The alarm clock danced around as the bell vibrated on the bedside cabinet. It must have been hammering away for over thirty minutes before there was a banging sound above from Mr Lacey. I'd have to pop up later to apologise. Luckily, I had laid out my suit and shirt last night, but for some reason I felt ravenous.

I started with orange juice followed by toast, which was my usual set-up for the day, but I needed eggs and bacon, so ended up having a full fry-up. I made a bacon roll for Mr Lacey and popped it up. His eyes lit up as I passed it to him, and he commented on how smart I looked.

I decided to catch the bus, I don't know why, but I felt so relaxed. The bus driver didn't charge me when I told him I didn't have the exact fare. A young guy gave up his seat for me. A woman made a fuss about some lint on the back of my jacket and began brushing it with her hand. She handed me a handkerchief, suggesting it matched my shirt and tie.

I got off the bus and walked slowly towards the office. I took the more scenic route and passed the racecourse and then paused to look up at two oak trees. In bygone years they'd been used for public executions.

When I reached HR, everyone was rushing around. A young guy on reception was talking on two phones. Behind him was a huge picture of Nula looking down smiling and in bold letters beside her face were the company's core values. She was framed with two faux peace lilies, their tones blending with her teeth.

A woman in a grey-checked suit with a blotchy complexion shouted across to another woman behind, who became flustered and dropped a stack of files. Two keyboard warriors sat bashing out their responses; one of them sighed and looked at the other shaking her head. A woman in her late fifties with scraped-back blonde hair and deep-set crevices under her eyes came out of a side room and looked me up and down. In all the years I'd been with the company, the only time I'd gone to HR was when I had to bring copies of my exam certificates. It was smaller and friendly then.

I felt like I was going through customs as I gave my name. I asked was there anywhere to sit as I couldn't see any seats. She asked whether I was ill. Eventually a chair appeared. One of the legs was bent which caused it to rock, so I abandoned it and stood watching the cacophony around me.

"I'm sorry but Nula isn't available today. Can you come back tomorrow?" The woman's crevices had softened. She apologised for the inconvenience and suggested another day that was mutually convenient. I made an appointment for the following week. For my reprieve, I would celebrate by going to the park. I'd go for a stewed tea at the café and maybe treat myself to a polystyrene sandwich.

Mr Brown Shoes hurried by and didn't look up, but he was mumbling. I wanted to get his attention but didn't know what I would say. It seemed inappropriate for me to do so. He stopped and looked around as he spoke on the phone. It was then I noticed his trousers. They had stains on them. They were bloodstains. He walked off, quickening his pace. I felt a compulsion to follow him; maybe he was hurt. I had developed a tacit bond with this guy.

I saw him hovering over near some rhododendron bushes, and then he disappeared. I got up and walked over to a metal obelisk. It was covered in ivy and partly obscured me as I stood watching. I saw him reappear a few minutes later. I followed. I walked past the café and saw the business suit sitting there reading the newspaper, but he kept looking over at the far side of the park. I followed his line of sight as he smiled at a woman doing exercises in one of the buildings opposite. He had a clear view, and she seemed not to mind while thrusting out her chest. He looked up, and I pretended to examine the blackboard listing the daily specials. The business suit turned his body in the direction of the woman, and then his hand moved to his crotch. I put my head down as I walked past and followed Mr Brown Shoes, who had disappeared through a wrought-iron gate into the rose garden.

It's not easy following someone. I could feel my heart pumping so fast and every time Mr Brown Shoes stopped, I darted behind something or tried to pin myself against a wall so as not to be seen.

He weaved through the patio area under the pergola and stopped. I turned and pretended to be talking into my mobile phone. I looked back and saw that he had gone through the far exit which led to the bus station. They were demolishing it to make way for a terminus, or at least that was the plan the town council had promised.

I followed and managed to get to the entrance of the bus station and saw him hovering near a skip. He looked around, and I threw myself behind a shrub. A bee hovered next to my face, looked at me and carried on. I peered from behind the bush and saw Mr Brown Shoes take something from under his jumper and throw it into the skip.

After looking around again, he leisurely strolled off. I watched him walk through the bus station and when I saw him disappear into a shop, I broke cover and walked towards the skip and leant across. It was full of rubble, concrete, broken chairs, toilets and washbasins. I even saw hypodermic needles and fast-food containers. I was about to reach in when I heard a loud beeping noise coming from behind; a truck started to reverse when two men jumped off. One of them waved his hand for me to move as the truck continued to back up. I wanted to see what was in the skip. I walked to the side and as I did so, I saw something. A knife covered in blood.

That evening, I was eating dinner when my phone flashed with a message from Charles: *Watch the news now!* I put the TV on and flicked through the channels when suddenly Nula's photograph appeared. I turned the sound up and moved closer.

"One of the top commercial directors in the country has gone missing. Nula Parry-Jones, forty-one years old, was last seen leaving Wracton Park Fitness Studio." The announcer went into detail about her achievements and described her as a warm, empathetic woman that everyone looked up to and that she was up for the regional Woman of the Year award.

The next day, the news gathered momentum. Nula's partner gave a press conference. In a strong Welsh accent he announced, "I miss her I do. I've been awful bard. It's my nerves, but if anyone has any news about my beautiful wife, please, please, I'm begging you to contact the police."

A senior police officer announced a fifty-thousand-pound reward, and a younger female police officer comforted Nula's husband and passed him a cappuccino.

"Ta, love." He winked.

Nula hadn't been seen for weeks. Her husband was wheeled out again and gave more interviews. He looked slimmer and more bronzed and wore a T-shirt with a photo of Nula along with a telephone number. He'd set up a charity for missing professional women. He cried as he sat clutching the woman police officer's hand.

The next day, I received a phone call from HR. They asked me to return to work. The disciplinary had been dropped and they looked forward to seeing me on Monday. I was surprised, speechless in fact, and when I returned, there was a different atmosphere. People were laughing and making jokes, my desk had been moved and there was a casserole from Tara.

"I thought I'd bring something nice to the table." She gave me a peck on the cheek.

I looked around. All the old processes had been reintroduced, and I saw Jenny back in the post room. She was singing. Eating at desks was allowed and lunch breaks were encouraged. Nula's office had been made into a chill-out room and a tea trolley introduced, and all the snack machines had been removed. In the reception area there was a plaque and a bronze figure of Theo with the inscription "Lest Not Forget".

As for Nula, the news reports gradually reduced to a small snippet here and there. There had been sightings and claims that her husband was having an affair and had done away with her. The patio was dug up and a sewer searched near their home, but nothing was found. The legacy of Nula's presence found its way to a skip.

It must have been two years later, when charred remains were found – quite by accident - in a landfill. The post-mortem identified them as Nula, and suggested that she had been stabbed and burnt alive. Apparently, it was a grisly death.

One newspaper suggested a satanic slant to it as though she was sacrificed. Another newspaper went into detail about the terrible torment and pain she had gone through. They are still running stories on Nula's death, and there was even an artist's impression of a suspect, which I looked at as I sat people-watching in the park.

I saw Mr Brown Shoes. He strolled by smiling as he talked into his phone. He looked at me and put his hand up. I did the same and smiled. I took another look at the artist's impression. It did look familiar.

Perhaps my friends are right ... I think too much and have an unhealthy mind to think such dark thoughts.

Out of Time

Lester stood admiring the town house shimmering in the sun. He took off his sunglasses and looked up at the blood-red geraniums cascading under the wrought-iron balcony, and then looked down to the road which led to the quayside lined with bistro bars and designer shops.

The years of training at medical school had paid off, and there was no more sleeping in dingy bedsits and eating takeaways. He'd borrowed heavily to buy into a GP practice, and the hours were punishing and the patients demanding, but as he took a step back, he looked up and he'd realised his dream.

The interior matched the opulence of the exterior, with the original plaster work and the beautiful fireplace with Delft blue tiles, which contrasted nicely with the black marble hearth. There were other additions, including a Victorian conservatory with Art Deco stained glass and the stripped pine floors that ran through all the reception rooms, and also the courtyard garden.

"Low maintenance." The brunette estate agent smiled. "They're after a quick sale and you've got to admit, it's a stunning house." She stood on the edge of one of the raised beds. "Look at that view."

Lester stood next to her and looked out at the sea and whistled. "Wow!" He took in a deep breath and shook his shoulders as he breathed out. "I'd like to put in an offer." He looked up at the sky and the circling seagulls. "But I can't match the asking price, Angie." He sighed.

"This is on the Q.T." she smiled. "But they're open to offers." She placed her hand on Lester's arm as she stepped down. "You're buying a piece of history. Do you know this used to be a smugglers' cottage?"

Jumping down, he asked, "Does it come with a parrot?" He stood on one leg.

"Straight up!" Angie laughed. "Look at the small window right up there." She stood on tiptoes pointing up towards the top of the house.

"The little indent thing up under the eaves?" Lester shielded his eyes as he looked up.

"That's where they used to hang a light which drew in the ships, causing them to smash into the rocks to their doom and killing everyone aboard."

"They'd run aground before getting anywhere near wouldn't they?" Lester surmised.

"We're talking of centuries ago, long before the dredging and building of the quayside." She looked up at Lester and smiled. "Pretty grisly goings on at Smugglers Cottage." She winked.

"I get it, it's part of the pitch." Lester laughed.

"It's history," Angie said with a shrug. "What can't talk can't lie." She gesticulated, pointing to the house.

Lester nodded as he did the sums in his head. "I'm willing to go to four hundred thousand. I can't go any further, and there's no point in—"

Angie held out her hand. "It's all yours."

"But it's way below the asking price." Lester's mouth dropped.

She took a pad out of her bag and wrote the price on the memorandum of sale.

"I can't believe it! Are you serious?"

Angie nodded as she continued writing. She paused and looked at Lester. "You were in the right place at the right time." She smiled and passed him the document.

Lester looked at it, and then punched his fist in the air. "Get in!"

"Welcome to Smugglers Cottage, Lester." She straightened her skirt. "You never know, you may find yourself some booty hidden within these walls." She winked. "Buyer takes all," she laughed.

A few weeks later Lester stood gazing into the empty house and the boxes he'd moved out of his bedsit. He had a few bits which looked tatty and out of place, so he'd been buying things off the internet. He'd bought a geometric orange lampshade and attached it to an olive-green base, which looked good on an Arts and Crafts side table. He'd upcycled a faux Le Corbusier leather couch from a friend; the chrome frame didn't look too bad displayed diagonally in one corner. It contrasted with the oriental rugs. He'd placed a large fern in the recess sitting in an earthenware pot, and church candles stood either side of the fireplace.

"There's something missing… You need this." Lester passed his friend Sadie a glass of Prosecco.

"Don't tell me, a standard lamp?" Sadie sipped the drink.

"No, something…"

She looked around the room. "Something…" She clicked her fingers. "Can't you hear?"

He followed her gaze. There was a child playing on a trampoline outside. "Oil for those springs or bloody earplugs?"

Sadie waved her hand. "No, silly. There is something missing from this room."

Lester looked at the walls. "Paintings. I know, a painting over the fireplace? I was thinking of a Rothko print. The colours would go well—"

"No, something befitting that has chimes."

Lester laughed. "A clock? I use my phone." He waved it above his head.

"No! A clock that fits in with the period... The sounds... The ambience."

Lester got a picture up of a clock on his phone.

"No, you idiot. I'd wish you'd be serious." Sadie pushed him away.

"Okay, I'll buy a clock. They have loads on the market, or I could get one of those projector thingy whatsits." He stood against the wall and spread out his arms pretending to be a clock.

"No!" Sadie snapped. "You need one with a beautiful mechanism that you wind up with pride. Just think of all the dedicated workmanship. You can't beat quality."

"A clock I wind up, great!" He searched his phone. "What about one that looks old but still has an app which I can control?"

Sadie took another swig of her drink. "No! A lovely walnut body and a brass mechanism." She was standing lost in thought. "Nothing too ornate, but not too plain, and no plastic." She looked over the images Lester had on his phone. "And not one of those hat boxes," she said, drawing an imaginary line in the air.

"Come again?" Lester followed Sadie as she walked around the room.

"You know what I mean. It's a sort of... It looks like... Who's the guy that did the Battle of Waterloo?"

"Napoleon?" Lester saluted.

"Yes." She walked over to the window. "Perhaps a bronze figure would be better," she suggested, looking down at the quayside. "You really have done well. I just can't get over how cheap you got this place."

Lester refilled her glass and looked at the mantelpiece. "You're right, Sadie. A clock it will be."

She clinked his glass. "Here's to Smugglers Cottage." They both toasted the house.

A crow sat on the window ledge watching. Sadie looked at it and shuddered.

"This place must have seen a lot of misery. I've read about houses retaining the memories and..." She looked at the crow as it craned its neck looking in. "And you said they used to lure the boats in?" Lester nodded. "Aren't you worried about all the...?" She looked at Lester and took another sip of her drink. "Murders and all the bounty they purloined? Just maybe it's left an impression in the house."

Lester laughed. "I've driven around the Santiago de Cali in Colombia and lived to tell the tale!"

Sadie shrugged. "But there wasn't a smugglers' cottage which was responsible for carnage, rape and pillage."

"Sounds like my kind of place." Lester shrugged, to which Sadie slapped his arm.

Lester led Sadie out onto the balcony and leant over, watching people walk by laughing and drinking outside the quayside bars. Sadie pointed to one couple.

"I went to college with her," she whispered. "I thought she'd married… or perhaps it was… or maybe it was… Yes, although I think she's now divorced." Lester nodded, but was confused with the thread of Sadie's conversation. "She plagiarised her final year project – then again, it may not actually be her." Lester nodded again as Sadie knocked back another glass of Prosecco.

"We've run out of time. I'm up at five. I'm on a surgical ward tomorrow."

She stood up. "Blimey, that's gone straight to my head. I feel so woozy."

Lester steadied Sadie and led her into the hall. "Next Saturday. A bit later as I've got to pop over to see Dad." He held the door open for the cab.

"I can see a light," said Sadie, looking up at the house. Lester turned, and then Sadie laughed. "Fooled you… Fooled you!"

Lester waved Sadie off, went back in and stacked the dishwasher and as he walked through the hallway, he saw a puddle of water shimmering in the light. He looked up and saw dripping. "Great…! I'm going to need to get that checked out."

The next day, a stocky plumber pulled down the attic ladder. "Old pipework can be a bugger to repair."

Lester held the bottom of the ladder. "I hope it isn't going cost too much, Nigel." Lester watched the thickset man climb the rickety aluminium ladder, which bowed under his weight. "How much are we talking about?" Lester watched Nigel's bulk disappear into the attic.

"All this plaster and the ceiling rose. A real bugger…" His voice disappeared.

Climbing the ladder, Lester poked his head through the attic hatch. "Sorry, I didn't hear what you said."

"Sorry, mate, difficult to tell until…" Nigel was shining a torch around. "It may be years of wear and tear." Lester switched on the light. "Cheers, much better." Nigel walked over to a large water tank in the far corner. "Hello." He grabbed one end of an aerial. "Not seen one of these in years. I hope you have cable." He chuckled. Nigel leant the aerial against a pile of black bin bags. "You see mate," Nigel stood hovering over the water tank, "this is where your leak is." He shone his torch. "Can you see it?"

Lester stood looking over Nigel's shoulder towards the torchlight hovering over a hole.

"The iron has corroded and over time, it's leaked onto the wood here." He pushed his sausage fingers into the rusty recess. "And the wood here has rotted. You can see the light down into the thingamabob." He shone his torch down through to the ceiling below and knelt down to take a closer look.

"How much will it cost?" Lester continued to look over Nigel's shoulder.

"A couple of hundred I reckon. Of course, there's the replastering." Nigel looked up at Lester. "It depends, although the water tank could be patched up." He stood up and raised his arm. Lester caught a waft of stale sweat. "It'll have to be drained first, and then there's the pressure in the heating system." He moved backwards and stumbled on something.

"Steady." Lester caught his arm.

"You've got a lot of stuff up here, mate. Once in the attic, it stays in the attic." Nigel laughed as he moved one of the bags and shoved it onto a box. He lost his footing and stumbled, falling backwards towards the chimney breast, dislodging a brick as he landed.

"Are you okay, Nigel?" Lester stepped over to help.

Nigel sat brushing the dust off his jacket. "Yeah, being a bruiser has its benefits. A bit of masonry work needed up here, mate." He looked up at where the brick had come away and shone his torch towards the wall, as another brick fell off.

"Watch it, please. I don't want your bill to increase," Lester joked as he went over to investigate, stepping over Nigel.

"I can cement this back in for you and…" The plumber shone his torch into the gap where the bricks had come away. "Wait a minute." He pushed in his sausage fingers. There was a clanking noise. "Hello." He passed the torch to Lester as he put in his other hand and pulled. They both looked as he retrieved an old box. Nigel tapped the side. "There's something in it." He pulled at the lip of the box and a musty smell filled the air. Lester sneezed. Nigel whistled. "Now, there's a beauty." Lester looked as Nigel lifted out a bronze head.

"A statue?" Lester moved forward and leant over to get a closer look.

"Yeah, I reckon so. Give me a hand."

Lester took one end. "Bloody hell, that's heavy."

They staggered over to the attic door. "If you go down first, I'll pass it down. We can lean it against the ladder. Hold it flush, mind," Nigel ordered. They managed to slide the box down the ladder. "One step at a time," Nigel called down as Lester's arms began to shake under the weight of the box.

Nigel carried the box to the dining table and slowly removed the bronze head. Lester stood back and looked at it. It had high cheekbones and eyes which looked oriental. Underneath was a clock face made of bronze with Roman numerals.

"That's definitely the most unusual clock I've ever seen." Nigel traced his fingers over the features with his fingers. "I'd do some research on that if I were you."

Lester nodded as he examined the mechanism. "Possibly 1800s or earlier," he suggested. "These Corinthian columns framing the face are of that period." He looked closer.

"Possibly copper plated, although I'd guess…" Nigel moved his fingers along the ridges. "Nah, it looks more like brass or something more precious." Looking at Lester, he added, "And it looks very expensive." Turning his attention back to the clock, he said, "Most unusual. I ought to charge you a finder's fee." He laughed while taking off the back. "Nice, a Swiss movement, probably added later, and not factory assembled if you look here." He pointed to the tiny screws and a signature. "Do you mind?" Nigel held up his phone and took some pictures. "I could get you a valuation if you like?"

Lester tilted the clock on its side and looked at the underside. There was a label coming away from the base written in bold copperplate-style writing. He knelt down and read, "Thou shalt not wind. I do beg…" But before he could read further, a strong breeze blew the label off towards the floor.

Nigel ran after it, stamping his foot down. "I've got it!" He stomped his size twelve foot on the floor, shaking a lamp on a side table. As he bent down to retrieve it, a strong breeze blew it from his grasp towards the balcony.

"Quick!" Lester shouted.

Nigel pushed his bulk out onto the balcony and lunged for the label, but it flew along and over the side down to the street below. They watched the label disappear towards the quayside.

"Hey, mate, get hold of that paper, please!" Nigel bellowed.

A man ran after it, but it blew away. The man looked back at Nigel and Lester. "Sorry, guys."

Nigel shrugged. "I wouldn't worry. Probably something about overwinding." He looked at Lester, who nodded.

"Probably Ye Old Lifetime Guarantee."

Nigel laughed. "It's worth a bit I'd say. Get it valued." He looked back towards the dining room table. "I'd say the clock is a good omen. Time stands still for no man." Nigel smiled as he looked down at his phone. "I'll ping you my quote." He looked up at Lester and smiled. "You'll find I'm very competitive." Nigel looked at the clock again and the woman's face. "A real beauty." Lester walked behind Nigel as he headed for the front door. "Just one thing…" He looked back and froze.

Lester frowned and said, "Are you okay?"

Nigel stared at the clock and pointed. "The eyes… they're open."

Lester turned and looked at the clock. The eyes were closed. He looked back at Nigel.

"They were open a few moments ago, I swear." He looked back at the clock. "She was looking right at me. I felt…" He broke off before leaving the house.

Lugging the clock over to the mantelpiece, Lester inserted the key into each hole, turning it anticlockwise until it wouldn't go any further. He then tilted it up on one side and gave it a gentle sway. He rested it down and stood back listening to the slow, melodic ticking. Sadie was right, the sound of a ticking clock added something to the house.

He looked at his phone. "Come on, my beauty, another five minutes and it'll be four o'clock." He stood mesmerised by the sound and the splendour of the bronze face. "Why hide such a thing? You must have been made for someone with money." He stood watching and examining the detail of the face, and then he checked his phone again. "One more minute." He looked up at the clock. "It will be fantastic if you work." He knelt down directly in front of the face. "Please chime." He watched as his phone counted down. "Another thirty seconds." Then it went to three, two, one. He looked at the clock and listened.

There was nothing at first, just the ticking, and then a new noise, the sound of ratchets drawing up, and then it chimed. The eyes opened and looked directly at him. One, two, three, four o'clock. And as soon as the clock finished, the eyes appeared to open wider and then they closed and the chiming ceased. Lester danced around the room as he called Sadie.

"I took your advice and invested in a clock."

"Oh my God. You actually took my advice, Lester." Sadie then went quiet.

"Are you still there?" He could hear her breathing.

"I hope it's not one of your silly gadget things. I'll throttle you if it is."

"No, of course not!" He blew a raspberry down the phone.

"How old and how much?" asked Sadie, munching on crisps.

Lester looked across at the mantelpiece. "I'd say 1800s – a bit before, give or take a decade or two." Sadie continued crunching. "How rude!" Lester said admiring the clock.

"I'm sorry. I'm having a quick break. It's mega busy here today. So, how much then, spill?"

He held the phone closer. "You still there?"

Sadie cleared her voice. "Yes, I wanted a drum roll!" she boomed down the phone.

"It was so much money."

Sadie took a sharp intake of breath, but before she could say anything, Lester burst out laughing.

"Zero pence." He looked over at the clock and winked.

"What do you mean zero pence?" Sadie's voice disappeared once again as she continued eating. "It's not one of those faux thingy whatsits which look baroque but are made in China and run off batteries?"

Lester patted the clock. "Come over and look for yourself."

A few hours later, Sadie was standing looking at the clock.

"In thirty seconds… Wait, you'll see." Lester looked at his phone and across at Sadie. "About now." He pointed to the clock. The mechanism began to ratchet up, and then the gong struck as the eyes shot open, looking directly at Sadie. On the last chime, the eyes widened, causing Sadie to shudder.

"She's looking directly at me… Did you see her eyes? I felt like she was staring into my soul!" She pointed. The eyes were now closed and the melodic tone filled the room.

"She's great, isn't she?"

Sadie frowned. "Unusual…" She examined the face closely. "I wonder how long she's been in the attic." She looked at Lester.

"I don't know – a few years."

Sadie traced her finger around the eyes and cheekbones. "Don't you have to contact the solicitors of the vendors?"

Lester wiped Sadie's fingerprints off with a handkerchief. "I signed a contract and all chattels and goods in this house are mine when it transferred into my name, so the clock is mine." Sadie stood watching Lester fuss over the clock.

"It's strange something so unique-looking and valuable would be hidden in an attic." She moved closer to him and whispered, "Do you think the pirates will try and reclaim their lost booty?"

"You were always the one who could put a sinister spin on things."

"No I'm not." Sadie poked Lester in the ribs. "But I find it's odd, that's all, for something," she looked at the clock again, "to be bricked in… That's what you said?"

Lester nodded. "Up in the attic. And this house was a smugglers' cottage. I can't see what other explanation there could be." Lester shrugged. "Allegedly, more in keeping with a holiday let." He patted the clock. "Probably to do with not declaring tax or a relationship breakdown. How much stuff do you have in the attic?" Sadie mumbled something. "Didn't quite hear."

"It's different for a woman. I have all my clothes and aside from that," she waved her hand, "I don't hide my stuff. There's something about her I don't like."

"Such as?"

Sadie walked around the mantelpiece. "She looks smug." She craned her head to look at her side-on. "No, more a resting bitch face." Lester snorted as he pushed his friend. "Oi!" Sadie ran after him.

"It's a piece of bronze inanimate metal, which makes a noise to announce the time, and it was your suggestion." Lester laughed as he ran out onto the balcony.

Sadie looked at the clock. "We'd better get going. The table is booked for seven-thirty." She looked at Lester. "I'm sure they can stretch to another chair if you want to bring madam along," she added, pointing to the clock. "And you can tell me more about this Angie." She said raising her eyebrow. "The estate agent."

Lester smiled. "She popped over today and brought me a house-warming present." He pointed to the bottle of champagne on the dining room table.

"I see. I suppose I'll be relegated to second division."

Lester put his arm around Sadie. "Don't be like that, but at least she liked the clock."

"Butter wouldn't melt, but under that hard exterior of metal there lies one jealous bitch," she said, gesticulating towards the timepiece.

That evening was hot and humid. Lester lay on top of the duvet with the windows wide open trying to get to sleep. Cats screeched outside and a dog barked as he tried to get comfortable. A car braked harshly followed by the shouting and screaming of a man and a woman arguing. He turned over drenched in perspiration and in the distance, the clock chimed before he felt himself drifting off.

Lester felt his body getting heavier as he fell into a deep sleep. He began murmuring while entering a dream state. His eyelids moved rapidly; he felt his body falling down through a mist. The mist cleared, and he could see the back of a woman walking over to a car holding her keys. He could hear the sound of her shoes against the pavement, and the jangling of keys. He watched her pause before pressing the key fob to open her car. There was a rustling sound coming from behind her. She turned and looked over to a bush and saw a small muntjac deer skip out. It momentarily looked and barked before scuttling off. She laughed reaching for the car door and as she was about to open it, a figure shot out from the bush and rushed towards her. She pulled the door open, but before she could get in, a figure grabbed her. She tried to scream, but a hand smothered her mouth as a blade plunged deeply into her throat. Her eyes widened as she fell to the ground.

Lester shot up. "Jesus!" He looked around the bedroom. All he could hear was the clock chiming, one, two, three, four o'clock, and then silence.

"A few new patients today." Brenda handed him the list, moved over, bent down and whispered, "Mrs Bexley's results." She paused as Lester leafed through the report.

He looked at Brenda and shook his head. "Will you show her in?" She touched his shoulder as she left.

"Hello, hello, Doc. What can I say? I've just had the most *fab-u-lous* holiday in Greece, look." Mrs Bexley twirled around showing off her tan. "And check these out." She pulled the chair closer to Lester and got out her phone. "The hotel was five stars." She scrolled through the pictures. "This is me and these are the girls and here is me by the pool." She clutched the phone to her chest. "I'm not wearing much." She smiled. "But then again, you've seen it all anyway." She nudged his arm with her elbow and laughed.

Lester continued to look at the picture. She looked good in the bikini and the reconstructive surgery was not noticeable.

"We've booked to go back next year. I can't wait."

"It looks a smashing place," Lester replied, smiling. He'd got to know her well over the years. She'd been quiet and unassuming at first, but became more vocal after the many trips to specialists to explore the pain and general fatigue, and then eventually the diagnosis.

"I've always wanted to go short," she'd said when she lost her hair.

"I've always wanted to go bigger," she'd announced when bloating following steroid treatment.

"Alphonso is doing well too." She'd sat back and smiled. "Just between you and me, he's my true love. We're soul mates," she'd added, clasping her hands together. "It's been two years and six weeks." She'd laughed.

Lester smiled as he remembered last year and the clear results and her discussing the future. But now he had to tell her as she reached her fifth year that the cancer had metastasised to her lungs. It was inoperable, and she had less than six months.

He looked at her as she continued to talk about upcoming events. *If only I could turn back time*, he thought, listening to her laughing.

"Having cancer was the best thing," Mrs Bexley had once said. "I had to get my priorities right, and he wasn't one of them," she'd declared when her marriage had failed.

After clearing his voice, Lester gave her the news.

She looked at him, attentively listening to every word, not asking any questions, and then she looked down at her shoes. "I think I'll get another pair." She looked up. "Let's face it, if it's bad as you say, I want to look my best." Lester could feel tears welling up. "Hey, Doc, I don't want you feeling sorry for me. Life is for living, and that's what I'm going to do." She got up and as she walked to the door, she turned and blew him a kiss. He returned the gesture.

Lester watched her leave and then listened to the raucous laughing in the waiting room. She brought laughter wherever she went. He banged his fists on the desk and kicked the wastepaper basket. Brenda popped her head around the door.

"You've got a thirty-minute break before the next one." She looked at him before adding, "I've just made some coffee." Lester followed Brenda into the back office, placed his hands on the table and breathed heavily. "Shocking news about that woman." Brenda passed him a mug of coffee.

"It never gets easy," he replied.

Brenda passed him a biscuit. "No, I mean the young woman murdered last night." She rubbed her arms. "It makes me go cold, and it was such a lovely evening and a stunning-looking girl too." She passed him the newspaper. "An estate agent." She pointed to a picture. "How cruel."

Lester felt sick as he stared at a smiling Angie in the photograph and the headline which read "Wrong Place at the Wrong Time".

Later that day, Lester met up with Sadie for dinner. "It's a coincidence – murders happen all the time. This is a big town, Lester," said Sadie, attempting to cut her steak.

"But I saw a woman being murdered in my dream – and then Angie, her throat cut just as I saw it."

Sadie chewed vigorously. "I thought it would be more tender than this." She gulped down some water and coughed. "That took some work!" She looked over at Lester, who was pushing his food around the plate. "It's the same as thinking about someone and then the phone rings. It happens to me all the time."

Lester stared at the food. "But you don't dream of someone being murdered, and then it happens!"

After beckoning over the waiter, Sadie said, "Another bottle, and the steak – it's not chef's best night."

"I'll get you another one," the waiter replied, looking at the plate of chewed morsels.

Sadie smiled. "I've read about a man dreaming of a plane crashing with red on its tip. A few days later, a plane with red on its tip crashed." She wiped her mouth. "It appeared he'd read about plane crashes and that the stats predict more crashes at that particular time of year with planes that have red on them or something along those lines…" Sadie held out her arm and touched Lester's hand. "You're an intelligent guy." He was looking down at his food. "Hey, you fancied her, didn't you?"

"We were meant to meet on Friday."

Sadie rested her hand on Lester's. "I'm so sorry, love. Life can be so cruel." She adjusted the sunglasses perched on her head. "You just don't know what's around the corner." Looking up, she said, "One of those slates could fly off that roof over there and hit my head. I could be perfectly fine, and the next day I could be talking away and keel over – a ruptured aneurysm, and that's me RIP." She sipped her wine. "And you know, estate agents meet lots of weirdos. Look at what happened to that poor girl in the 1980s. They never found her." Lester knew Sadie had a point. "You're mourning the loss of opportunity, Lester." Sadie topped up his glass. "Let's celebrate Angie's life." She held up her glass high. "To you, my darling." Lester followed suit and looked upwards to the clear night sky. "And I hope they catch the bastard. I certainly won't be walking anywhere at night." She took another sip of her wine and whispered, "I wonder if it's someone she knew."

It was another hot and humid evening, so Lester had dampened a towel and placed it on top of his duvet. It was something an old Spanish lady had advised him when he was staying in Córdoba. The heat had been unbearable and the landlady of the pension had, through various arm movements, demonstrated to Lester the art of staying cool during the night.

His body was cooler and he began drifting off. The sounds outside began to fade as his eyes began flickering and his body twitched entering the dream state.

He could see a house surrounded by fields. It was the most beautiful afternoon, and two small children and a dog were playing in a large garden. There were apple trees and other fruit trees and a stream. The children ran down towards the water laughing as a woman wearing a headscarf waved after them. She was carrying a basket and headed towards the apple trees singing to herself. A summer breeze rippled around the branches and a wind chime sounded in the distance. A figure stood next to a bush watching the woman gathering the apples. The children were in the stream throwing a stick for the dog, which barked and wagged its tail retrieving it. The woman sang to herself as the figure moved closer, and then there was the sound of a branch cracking.

"Have you finished already?" The woman was still singing and slowly turned around.

A metal blade caught the reflection of the sun as it plunged into her throat. She fell to the ground like a rag doll. The clock began chiming one, two, three, four.

Lester sat bolt upright, screaming.

"You've been working too hard, that's all. Nightmares are a sign of stress." Sadie patted his hand. "Buying this house and the GP practice and all the hours over the last few years have taken its toll. Stress is a slow burner… You need a holiday – a nice break to take you away from things."

Getting up, Lester walked out to balcony. "These aren't bad dreams – these are real! I felt like I was there. The woman last night, I saw her being killed, as I did Angie…" He looked down to the quayside. Sadie put her arm around him.

"I know, but you only knew it was Angie when Brenda told you. It's a coincidence – and the woman last night, don't you see it's a similar theme because it's stress?" Lester slouched, resting his arms against the balcony. "I didn't mean to trivialise what you're saying. I still think you need some time off."

"It felt so real. Someone has been killed. I just know it." He took a deep breath.

Sadie watched Lester look at her. "Promise me, please, take some time off. Stress does your head in. Trust me."

"Okay." Lester wiped his eyes and nodded. "I'll take a couple of days off. I'll go and see Alex and the boys and travel around."

"Make it a couple of weeks." Sadie gave him a kiss. "You've not been away for the last couple of years. She'll be glad to see you. Promise me you won't go back on your word." Lester did a sign of the cross. "Good. I can check on here if you want. Water the plants and wind madam up." She looked across at the clock.

A few days later, Lester headed down to the coast towards Ilfracombe. His sister had moved there from London following her divorce.

"Hello, mister. Nice to see you after three years." Alex wrapped her arms around him.

"Life just takes over. It's always difficult to find time. You know how it is."

Alex led him into the farm kitchen. "Rhubarb crumble, and I've made an assortment of pies." Lester looked over at the Welsh dresser at all the pies lined up. "This one is damson – a bit tart but lovely with a lashing of sugar. There are savoury ones here, cheese and onion, steak and kidney, and a lovely apple one here, too." Lester rubbed his hands as Alex served a huge helping of the rhubarb and apple pie.

"Where are the boys?"

Alex drizzled on some mascarpone. "Tell me when. They're at their dad's. Good timing in a way as I need to go to London next week."

"That's enough!" Lester touched her arm. "I'll be getting high cholesterol!" They both laughed. "I'll stay a couple of days and go around the coast." Alex sat next to Lester.

"It's so good to see you, and you can stay as long as you want. Jack and Jon will want to see you. Swing by on your way back." She served up another helping. "Tell me about your new house and how's the world going in GP Land?" Lester took his phone out and scrolled through the photos. "Wow, that looks a stunning place." Alex looked on as Lester gave her a running commentary with each photo.

"This is my lounge. I've had the floor sanded and buffed up to a new colour."

Alex nodded, and then touched his arm. "Wait a minute. Just go back and zoom in there." She pointed to something over by the mantelpiece. "The clock – she's a beauty." Alex stared at it. "It's unusual…"

"Late Victorian or early twentieth century," he replied, nodding.

"It looks much older than that." Alex looked closer. "And the eyes, they're so creepy."

"It must be the light."

Walking over to the worktop, Alex asked, "Another cuppa?" Lester nodded. She then switched on the radio and stood listening to a love song. She smiled as she got out two mugs.

Three beeps sounded. "The main news headlines in the south of England. Police are investigating the murder of a woman…"

"Can you turn it up?" Lester quickly asked.

"Lesley Harrington was found by her two children with her throat cut. They are being comforted along with her husband, Nigel, a local plumber…"

Lester cut short his visit and headed back home. The town was full of tourists, so he had to abandon his car in the next street. He ran weaving between people as they stood outside shops and congregated outside bars and restaurants. One man stood in front of his house taking a picture of the blood-red geraniums hanging over the balcony. Lester pushed past as he ran into his house and headed for the clock. It was gone. He ran around banging doors shouting for Sadie. He returned to the lounge and saw a note propped up against a vase of freshly cut flowers. He recognised the pink swirly writing.

Welcome home! I want to hear everything about your travels. I'll pop over tomorrow. Everything went well apart from the clock – the mechanism is jammed. Can't wait to catch up. Love Sadie xx.

He phoned her straight away. It went straight to voicemail. "It's me. The clock, where is it?"

Lester paced as he continued to call Sadie. "Please pick up!" he shouted down the phone.

Grabbing a bottle of vodka, he poured himself a drink and then another. He continued to pace as he knocked back the drinks until he grabbed his car keys and decided to drive over to Sadie's.

As he drove across town, the traffic was at a standstill. It was tourist season. He shot down a side street and rejoined the main interchange. A car in front stalled. Lester thumped his fist on the horn. The car started and lurched forward as the lights changed. Lester pushed his foot hard on the accelerator and shot through the lights. A car coming from the other direction turned sharply as Lester hit it, causing the car to collide into a parked van. Lester banged his head on the steering wheel. Shortly after, blue lights engulfed his car.

The cell was cold. Lester curled up in a ball and pulled a threadbare blanket over him. He was exhausted, and had been arrested for being over the limit. He could hear laughter and shoes tapping loudly down the long corridors. And then silence, apart from the ratcheting sound of a clock. Then the gong struck and the eyes opened. One, two, three, and on the last strike the eyes widened momentarily as the blade slashed across the neck of a woman.

Lester shot up screaming. Footsteps came running down the corridor with the clanking of keys as the door sprang open. Lester sat shaking. "Blood! Knife. A woman. She's dead!" he screamed, running up to the police officer.

"You're lucky they didn't push for a blood test, but they could see you were in a bad way." His solicitor passed him a sheet to sign. "You'll have to appear before the magistrates I'm afraid, but with your standing as a GP and the stress you've been under, you should be able to keep your licence. Go and get some rest – you look terrible."

Lester got a cab to his GP practice. When he arrived, Brenda was standing out front.

"I'm sorry, Lester. It's just awful," she said, looking at him getting out of the cab in a crumpled shirt and his hair sticking up. Brenda steadied him. "You should go home. It's too much of a shock."

"I'll have a shower — " Lester waved his hand, "— and it will take an hour to fix myself up." He looked at Brenda, his eyes bloodshot. "I'll be fine." He could see tears in Brenda's eyes.

"Please get back in the cab. It's too much, Lester. Sam will call by later and give you something." Lester pushed Brenda away.

"What are you talking about? I-I was over the limit. I forgot I'd drank, that's all." Lester stumbled. Brenda tried to help, but he pushed her away as he made his way into reception. He looked around at the patients sitting looking up at Lester. One boy pointed at the television screen and a picture of Sadie and the words "Woman Butchered". Lester moved forward. His vision became blurred as he stumbled, and then everything went black.

A light flickered and Lester focused his eyes. He heard the sound of a machine beeping next to him and felt a plastic tube sticking out of his arm.

"There you go now. You've had us worried, to be sure." An elderly nurse looked down smiling. "Will you be wanting anything to eat? Chef has quite the menu." Lester struggled attempting to sit up. "Be careful now – you've fractured a shoulder and got a nasty gash." She placed her hand behind his back, to which Lester cried out in pain. "Too much? Steady back down, and I'll place another pillow behind. Small steps now; don't do too much."

Lester spent the days looking out of the window.

"You'll have to eat something. Chef has prepared this for you." The nurse placed down a tray of steamed salmon and seasonal vegetables. "He's made you a beautiful hollandaise sauce. Now don't disappoint us, will you?" She smiled seeing Lester lift himself into a sitting position.

Brenda popped her head around the door. "I thought you'd like this. Dr Michael will be calling in later. He'll help you back home." She looked around the room at the cards and flowers and smiled. "But only when you're ready." She pulled up a chair. "Don't worry about coming back, not until you're ready. We'll get a locum." Brenda smiled. "Take each day as it comes. Time is a great healer."

"I want to go home. I need to get back into a routine." Lester continued to stare out of the window.

The blood-red geraniums hung over the wrought-iron balcony. The house looked pristine. The white rendering shimmered in the summer daylight and the door was freshly painted.

"We thought we'd tidy things up. Alex helped but had to go back to see the boys." Brenda helped Lester out of the cab. "She came to see you a number of times, but you were always asleep." She opened the front door and bent down to gather the post as she helped Lester over the step, making sure she didn't knock his shoulder.

"I want to sit over there."

Brenda helped him into the lounge. "Dr Michael will come in later to see how you are. I've also got a lady coming in to help you this evening, and you'll have someone in the morning and…"

"My carers, you mean." Lester smiled.

Standing with her hands clasped together, Brenda replied, "Just for a couple of weeks until you're back on your feet. I've organised a weekly grocery delivery, and the fridge and cupboards are full. And I'll pop over first thing." She leant over and gave Lester a peck on the cheek.

Lester felt a breeze across his body, and then someone pulled a blanket over him. There were hushed voices, followed by footsteps and sound of the door being closed. As he drifted deeper into sleep, the quayside began to come alive with the bars serving groups of people. Laughter and music filled the night air. Lights around the quayside filled the night sky. A wind chime sounded in the distance, as did the call of a bird.

A crow sat on the windowsill. Lester opened his eyes. He could hear a clock. He struggled to sit up and saw the clock on the mantelpiece; the eyes were open as it began to chime.

A figure stood in the shadows by the doorway. Lester swung his legs round and pulled himself up. As the clock sounded the last chime and the eyes widened, a blade plunged down.

Nearby, a magpie dropped a scrap of paper. It rolled along the pavement until an elderly lady trapped it with her foot. She picked it up and read out loud, "Thou shalt not wind. I do beg of thee, or thou shalt run out of time."

The Disturbance

Strange things had been happening at St Swithin's Mews.

It was a row of town houses dating back to the 1920s, which in their time were resplendent apartments with balconies to the front and back, and once formed part of an exclusive development for the nouveau riche. Sadly, their exteriors, now tarnished with the passage of time, sat in the middle of a mishmash of social housing and retail developments that had sprung up over the decades. St Swithin's was incongruous and to add to its uniqueness, the houses ran in odd numbers, often confusing visitors. However, there was one thing that everyone agreed on, the occupants of St Swithin's Mews all had something in common: they were odd.

Mrs Spelter had lived at number one St Swithin's Mews for over thirty years. She was a woman of means after inheriting from her father and busied herself supporting local charities, with her photograph often appearing in the local newspaper smiling as she opened fetes and annexes to new buildings or organised events to support any number of good causes.

She had recently joined the trends on social media and regularly posted updates of what she was doing throughout the course of the day. This gave her the opportunity to show off her expensive clothes, jewellery and hairstyles. Of course, she knew how to filter and shave off the odd chin or two. Sadly, she couldn't apply technology to her image in real life. The years were less forgiving, as her face bore a striking resemblance to that of a steam pudding, with two raisins for eyes, and her figure more carthorse than wood nymph.

Something strange was happening in St Swithin's Mews, and it all started on Friday night when a noise awoke Mrs Spelter. At first, she thought it was somebody kicking a can or bottle in the road. She had complained and written to local newspapers describing the disrespect of the modern youth, who congregated at one of the many late-night shops, selling what she termed "uncouth items", such as cheap alcohol and the emergency contraception pill. She turned over but before her head even touched the pillow, there was a loud crash coming from downstairs. She pulled the sheets up to her neck as she sat bolt upright listening to the intruder. The crashing continued, so she moved one arm under her black satin valance, fished out the golf club she kept under her bed and sat watching the door.

The sound was moving along the hallway towards the stairs. Hearing creaking floorboards, she leant across to switch on the side lamp and stealthily moved out of bed, still clutching the golf club tightly to her chest. She took a few deep breaths and on the last one held the golf club out in front and let out the loudest shriek you could imagine. Bolting out of the bedroom waving the club above her head like Queen Boudicca, she ran along the landing and continued screaming and swinging the club from left to right, searching the hallway through to the lounge, study and dining room.

The echo was deafening as she crashed around with the tenacity of a poltergeist, banging every door and switching on every light. But there was nothing. She continued her rampage screaming at the top of her voice, "I've called the police, you thugs!" But still she found no intruder or night creeper hiding behind a door or lurking in the shadows.

Her wailing gave way to a whimper and after her reconnaissance, she collapsed onto the sofa exhausted. She caught her breath before grabbing the telephone which sat on a malachite-topped occasional table, and called the police.

"There's more than one I'm sure, and I'm a lone female." She sat looking across the lounge at her beautiful ornaments lying smashed on the floor. She picked up the decapitated head of a cherished cat ornament and cried. And then through her tears, she saw red paint dripping from the back of the lounge door. Heartbroken, she walked across and carefully pushed the door with the slightest of touch. She instantly screamed.

There written in the same red paint was the word denouncing her as a "Whore".

She ran to the kitchen and frantically opened her cupboards, pulling out all the cleaning products and tossing them into a bucket. The doorbell rang and she heard voices. Wailing, she hurried to the defaced door and started scrubbing.

"It's the police!" a man's voice shouted.

Mrs Spelter shoved the bucket and cleaning products into one of the cupboards in the hall and kicked it shut, and then rushed into the lounge and propped open the door so it was flush against the wall before running to the front door and collapsing into the arms of one of the policemen.

One of the police officers helped the distraught Mrs Spelter over to the sofa and offered to make her a cup of tea.

"Earl Grey," she requested, languishing and withering in torment. "Perhaps a couple of the macaroons – third cupboard along and in a tin on the second shelf," she croaked.

"Are you up to providing a statement?"

Mrs Spelter nodded and described in great detail the day's events and the new outfit she'd worn.

"Perhaps if we concentrate on what you heard and whether you saw anything out of the ordinary," one of the officers suggested as he scribbled to keep up.

Mrs Spelter gesticulated, her arms flailing outwards while describing the events of her feeling hopeless with death hanging over her. "I'm on tablets you know," she declared. "I'm exhausted – it's the adrenaline." Then, Mrs Spelter slumped forwards.

One of the officers helped her up. He was young and athletic, and for some reason she felt faint.

"It must be delayed shock." She grabbed one of his biceps as her breast brushed against his arm. "You're so kind. This whole experience has been purgatory." She pulled his arm closer.

Another officer collected the shards of glass and china when he noticed the red paint marks dripping from the back of the lounge door. Mrs Spelter shot a horrified look as the officer removed the doorstop. He smirked.

Mrs Spelter's eyebrows rose as she bellowed, "What are you going to do about this?" She pointed to the door, her eyebrows meeting her hairline. "This is obviously one of those reprobates from over there." She turned on her heels and pointed in the direction of the adjoining council estate. "Most of them don't work, but they come and break into innocent houses daubing such vile abuse." Her voice raised an octave as she shrilled, "That nasty, nasty word!" She drew herself even closer into the young police officer's chest. "Please help me to my room. I've never experienced such filth!" she wailed as the officer escorted her to the bedroom.

Mrs Spelter had a history. She'd incurred many parking tickets, but had somehow swayed the parking adjudicator that she was an innocent victim. "It's these hot flushes. The sweats go down one side and across the other and then down my back." She went into further details on the forms she submitted, which ran to several pages. "And the brain fog – I don't know if I'm coming or going. The yellow just blurred, and I thought it was…"

The magistrates heard a similar story when she was booked for parking in a bus lane. "The buzzing in the fingertips. It's no wonder I have to stop and get out. They should build more hard shoulders for women like me afflicted with such a debilitating disorder," she'd complained.

And there were the anonymous calls which couldn't be verified of a man who maintained he'd been assaulted by Mrs Spelter. "Rubbish! It is I who was assaulted!" she'd proclaimed, thrusting out her chest in indignation. The younger man didn't want to give evidence, but did allude to the fact that he'd met a woman claiming to be in her early thirties who looked similar to Mrs Spelter on a dating website. The police had been approached by a number of other young men describing being petrified by a woman they'd met online, but they refused to give further details.

The disturbance at Mrs Spelter's put her on the front page of one of the local newspapers. She asked her cleaner to buy extra copies. "My friends will insist." It was a good picture – a professional photo taken ten years previously.

"You've got to give her credit. She knows how to strike a pose. You can hardly see her double chins," Althea said, passing the newspaper to her husband.

Althea and Seb lived at number three St Swithin's Mews. Althea continued to read.

"They caused over twenty thousand pounds' worth of damages." She whistled. "Poor old Valerie. We'll have to pop round." She applied another layer of marmalade to her toast.

"I expect it's one of those from across the estate. Revenge for her campaign against the regeneration and shoving them out in the sticks," Seb said as he texted.

"Perhaps, but her house is a fortress."

Seb looked up and laughed. "Yeah, any poor soul who gets in won't be able to leave."

Althea gave her husband a withering look. "She's not that bad. Although, I don't know what they would steal as the newest thing she has is a Spode dinner service circa 1935."

"Now who's being catty?"

Althea ignored her husband's comment. "I had another one of my strange dreams. I felt someone sitting on my chest. It wasn't you was it?" Althea looked across at her husband, who was still texting. "Seb, it wasn't you?" He looked up.

"No, I went out like a light."

"I felt something around my neck." She sat pondering as she recollected her dream. "And a strange taste."

"Too much of that," Seb suggested as she layered more marmalade on the toast. "Acid reflux," he added before leaning across and grabbing the last piece of her toast.

That night, Althea struggled to sleep. She turned one way and then the other, and eventually got out of bed and headed for the kitchen to make a cup of tea. But still she couldn't drop off. Reluctantly, she headed for the bathroom cabinet and reached for a bottle she'd hidden behind a large jar of facial scrub. She examined the date and knocked back a couple of sleeping tablets she'd been prescribed years earlier. Seb didn't approve of sleeping tablets or anything the GP dispensed. "They are just legalised drug pushers," he often declared. But they worked and Althea began drifting off but, in the distance, she heard noises.

Her body was succumbing to the effects of the drug and as she drifted deeper, she felt something around her neck. She couldn't breathe; was choking. The sleep paralysis made it impossible for her to move. She was going to die. Her body contorted as she struggled, and then Seb moved and the grip loosened. Althea sat up screaming.

"Someone was strangling me!" She leant forward taking deep breaths, swung her legs out of bed and stood up. Her pyjamas fell to the floor as she stumbled into the bathroom to splash her face with water. She looked in the mirror. "Oh my God, my neck! Seb, my neck, look!"

Her husband ran in to see what all the commotion was about and saw the large red wheals around Althea's neck. He examined them closely. "Are you sure you've not had something round there?"

Althea shook her head. "I felt someone strangling me, Seb. Someone was trying to kill me." She burst into tears as Seb helped her to the side of the bath where he wet a towel with cold water and wiped her face and neck. "And my pyjamas – I double knotted them. I don't understand how they came undone. And my knickers – they've gone." She looked at her husband. "Seb?"

"Darling, I don't know what's happened…" He shook his head.

Later that night the police were called to number five, where Tyrone Hamilton lived with his two children, Sabrina and Freya. Freya awoke crying because she saw somebody in her bedroom.

The children's toys lay decapitated. One of the teddy bears had been strung up by its neck, and a couple of dolls had their legs and arms snapped off. Graffiti was daubed across the wall of the downstairs toilet describing Mr Hamilton as a pervert, and there was more graffiti on the back door proclaiming that he "was in the closet".

"It's not true," Mr Hamilton said softly, looking down at the floor.

He and his children attended church regularly and were known to give up their free time for good causes.

The police officer took down his statement. He handed him a stack of magazines with naked men on the covers. "I found these."

"They're not mine, Officer. I don't know who would do such a thing. I've not done any harm to anyone." He turned towards his daughters, who ran crying to their father and hugged him.

A leaflet drop was carried out by the police to all the residents of St Swithin's Mews.

Michael Tarlington was a recruitment consultant who lived at number seven, which he'd occupied for just under two years. He'd wanted one of the larger executive houses, but that fell through after being gazumped. He was rarely in and had considered putting the house up for sale. "I'd hardly get a good price now," he complained when speaking to one of the police officers. "No, I haven't seen or heard anything suspicious, and I rarely see my neighbours."

Mr Tarlington used number seven as a drop-off point. He was an orderly man with few possessions. Everything was white, he had a long clothes rail with several suits all labelled, and he had an expensive television with surround sound.

"I have an alarm system that I set each time I'm away." His brother-in-law minded the house when he wasn't at home. "Yes, I can give you his details. He stays here a couple of times a month, more out of necessity as he works nearby." The police officer took down all the particulars.

Ms Gladstone-Davies lived at number nine. A woman of uncertain years who had worked as a buyer for a local fashion house, but was now retired. She still worked the odd day at a local designer outlet on a strictly ad hoc basis.

"No, Officer, I've not seen anything except what I read in the newspaper. Those poor little girls of Mr Hamilton. Freya comes over – I'm helping her design a couple of outfits for one of her dolls."

She had many hobbies, one of which was to enter competitions. Her house was full of the prizes she'd won including a new Chesterfield sofa and dining suite as well as a utility room well-stocked with cleaning products.

"My signature win is these," she said as she showed the police officer her chest freezer stacked with steak, loins of pork, brisket and more Scottish salmon than any restaurant in town could better. "Of course, it's a dreadful worry. I pop in to see Mr Santiago. He's an invalid but a sweet man. Yes, Officer, I'll make sure the locks are on, and I do have window locks. No, I don't have an alarm. I may well look into having one fitted now." She showed the police officer to the front door.

There was graffiti smeared across one of the shop's shutters denouncing the occupants of one of the council estates as jobless trash.

One of the police officers looked across at St Swithin's Mews. "I wonder if one of them is getting their own back."

A couple of the council estate residents had complained of smashed windows. One occupant had had her window boxes flung across the road.

"Probably separate incidences, but log them, won't you?" the duty sergeant instructed.

Another neighbour at a housing association found two of her garden gnomes performing sex acts over her oriental pond. "Kids I expect – it is that time of year," one of the officers commented. So more officers covered the beat.

"This was always such a nice area. Something strange is happening and I don't like it," one of more senior officers remarked as he stood looking up at St Swithin's Mews. "This was one of the best places to live in Northamptonshire, the playground of the rich and famous, and now all this antisocial behaviour." He shook his head.

Henri Santiago lived at number eleven St Swithin's Mews. He was an elderly man who lived alone apart from the carers who came in each day to wash and dress him. He liked to look well-groomed and wore a vibrant neckerchief, silk-lined jackets and a Fedora, and he smoked cheroots. Sadly, his mobility had reduced because he was crippled with arthritis; he took morphine to ease the pain.

He would often sit on one of the balconies watching everyone walk by. "A beautiful day," was his usual greeting to anyone who ventured past. "It will rain this afternoon. Never cast a clout until May is out," he'd say if he saw anyone not dressed appropriately for the weather.

Henri held up a sherry glass while dispensing his pearls of wisdom. He had an exotic past. He had dated film actresses when dipping his foot into show business. "One or two films, darling," he would modestly attest. He'd dated some of the most famous and rolled off many names.

Althea would gush and look at him in awe but given the age gap, she struggled putting faces to the names. "Gosh, Henri, you were a one." He'd wink.

"I certainly was. Of course, did I tell you I was a body double for...?" He would reel off even more names. He had light blue eyes and upon closer inspection, you'd see that one of his pupils was larger. "A blown pupil as they often call it." He would smile. "It's very lucky. Something I inherited from the male side of the family." He'd wink again.

In his later years, Henri Santiago had become more creative and worked in the theatres in Paris. He'd created visual backdrops and costumes, and the walls of his house were adorned with old masters and impressionist paintings with many photographs hemmed in between of him pictured with some famous movie star. The high ceilings contrasted with vibrant walls, each room themed and splashed with colours ranging from heritage green, scarlet red, burnt orange to burgundy. Huge plaster ceiling roses held glass-cut crystal lampshades which dazzled when lit. He made sure one of his two cleaners dusted them thoroughly every few weeks.

"Appearances are important, and you must not let yourself go, no matter what," was his mantra to anyone who visited. He used a wheelchair, but found it difficult due to the wasting of his arm muscles. "You can't complain. There are people a lot worse off."

Ms Gladstone-Davies clasped her hands. "He's a marvel!" she declared to one of his carers when she popped in to see if he wanted anything. He enjoyed knowing what was going on.

The police advised him to increase his security, and his carers were instructed to ensure further locks were fitted and an alarm installed linked to a monitoring station.

The disturbances at St Swithin's and the surrounding estate subsided. Senior police officers were happy. "One-off probably – some local creeper who's been banged up. Keep up the regular visits, and we'll review in four weeks."

After four weeks, the police were stood down from the case and things went back to normal. Mrs Spelter opened more garden fetes and championed good causes. Althea's tearoom was busy catering for the tourist season. Henri sat on his balcony waving and chatting as he smoked his cheroots. He had an easel set up and began sketching a picture of the view of the rooftops.

"You're so talented, Henri. I wish I had half of your gifts," Althea said, admiring his sketches.

But the silence over St Swithin's would be shattered once again.

It was that night when the disturbance returned to number one. Mrs Spelter returned home after a night out with a gentleman friend. She hadn't noticed at first, but her watch had stopped and when she checked the time against her grandfather clock, she noticed that the hands were missing and the word "slut" was written across the front and there were scratch marks up the body of the clock.

"Look here, something dug here and here," one of the police officers said to his colleague. "Looks like a screwdriver or some other sharp instrument."

His colleague knelt down and looked more closely. "That's odd. They look like tracks." He inspected it further. "Yes, a small object or thing has climbed that." He looked around at Mrs Spelter sat on the sofa sobbing.

"Is there nothing sacred?" she wailed, clutching one of the younger officer's arms.

The disturbance was continuing at St Swithin's. At number three, Althea couldn't stomach any more marmalade.

"You've overdone it," Seb said. He looked at his wife, who had turned an ashen colour, and then she bolted out of her chair and headed for the bathroom. He could hear her vomiting. A couple of minutes later, he poked his head around the door. "I've brought you a mint tea."

She looked up forlornly kneeling by the toilet. "I feel so ill." She then turned her head to the basin and vomited again. Seb helped his wife back to bed. She couldn't keep anything down and was too poorly to go into work, so Seb arranged for one of her managers to oversee the business.

There was a pattern to her vomiting and after a gentle prod from her husband, she reluctantly went to see her GP.

"I felt something sitting on my chest, and look…" She opened her top and showed the GP tiny pinpricks across her chest.

The GP instructed Seb to pick up the prescription and ordered his patient home to bed.

Seb returned laden with gifts and treats along with the prescription. "Althea!" he called as he put the bags down on the hall table. "How are you feeling?" he called while popping into the downstairs cloakroom to use the toilet. On his way to the bedroom, he tripped over Althea's handbag. "Althea, you there?" He found his wife sobbing, sitting on the floor, her head perched on the side of the bed in the spare bedroom. "Hey, you. I've been looking for you. What's up?" He knelt down and hugged her.

She looked at him. "I'm pregnant."

Seb didn't register what she'd said at first. "What?"

"I'm pregnant, Seb." She continued looking at him and sobbing.

"Pregnant?" he repeated. She blew her nose. "But… how?"

"I'm not going to give you a biology lesson now, you bloody idiot." She burst into uncontrollable tears.

"But you can't be." He hugged her while staring into space. "I just don't understand… My testosterone levels… You've not—"

Althea slapped his face. "Whatever you're thinking, karma will get you for that, Seb!"

He clung to her tightly. "Why are we so miserable? We should be shouting it from the rooftops." Althea looked at Seb and wiped her eyes. He then jumped up and down. "You see why I don't trust the medical profession. It must have been a few weeks back when I was taking all those herbal remedies." He gave his wife's tummy a gentle pat.

The same day Ms Gladstone-Davies reported she had seen a shadow walk past her property. "It was yesterday, yes definitely yesterday."

The police officer looked at her. "Are you sure, madam?" She nodded.

"Yes, Officer, I am."

And so it was established that there was a creeper lurking about St Swithin's Mews causing menace and mayhem.

Number three had reported it, too. Althea thought she saw something walk along the balcony. "It may have been a cat," she'd suggested.

"I want to catch whoever it is. I want a mobile CCTV unit put up outside for a couple of hours each night. And bugger the cost!" the chief inspector shouted.

Mr Henri Santiago sat watching from his balcony. "It reminds me of when I was a stunt double." He described in detail when he abseiled down a building as explosive charges were let off. His new carer sat listening to every word.

"Wait till I tell my mum. Can I take a pic of you, Henri, on my phone?" Mr Santiago obliged and posed against the photographs of some of his famous actor friends.

Mr Hamilton at number five woke up in agony. The paramedics were called, and he was rushed into A&E. The foreskin of his penis had been glued shut.

He underwent emergency surgery; a catheter was inserted to ease his discomfort.

"This is barbaric!" the chief inspector bellowed as he slammed his fist on the desk. "Have you questioned everyone?"

His second in command nodded. "Any truth in him with other…?"

The officer shook his head. "No, sir. He likes women, and we've interviewed all of them."

The chief inspector uncrossed his legs.

Mr Harlington was interviewed a few days later. He was drowsy and still in great distress. "I remember something on my leg." He rubbed his head. "I moved, and then felt something on my thigh and then a pain. I turned over. I heard something on the floor – a tapping sound. I thought it was a cat."

The police officer typed up the statement.

"We're going to have to add GBH. What the hell is going on in that place? I want background checks on everyone. I want a sweep of all past offenders regardless of their modus operandi within the area," the chief inspector demanded. "I need this solving ASAP." He kicked his foot against the desk. He'd taken this post as it was a more genteel town and now here, he was dealing with a creeper, a sexual pervert and wanton vandalism. He'd promised his wife that he would retire in twelve months. "I need this solving!" he shouted.

Things appeared to settle down once more at St Swithin's. The measures put in place by the police were working, but still there were no arrests. The fete on the green was held every August – an occasion Mrs Spelter referred to as the "wow factor". She worked hard to bring the community together and given the events of the last five months, extra effort was incorporated with many of the occupants of St Swithin's helping out.

Mr Santiago volunteered to draw portrait pictures for a modest fee. Althea would donate some of her deli treats. Ms Gladstone-Davies worked on the backdrops and costumes for the play. The committee decided on *A Midsummer Night's Dream*. Freya and Sabrina would be wood nymphs. Mrs Spelter volunteered to be Titania, and Seb was to be her Bottom, although he refused to go around to her house for late-night rehearsals without a chaperone.

The fete was well attended and there was high praise for the performers, although Althea had to prompt Titania several times as she wailed excitedly looking for her next line. Mr Santiago sat painting a frieze, which was later put up for the raffle. And so, the inhabitants of St Swithin's were getting back to some sort of normality and had raised a considerable amount of money.

"Publicity pays," Mrs Spelter said, examining the takings once more. "We've trebled our target."

The media swooped, and Mrs Spelter posed for several pictures, including one of her kicking up her leg.

The quietness would not last for long. The disturbance returned. This time with far worse consequences.

Mr Tarlington arrived home to number seven; he'd be on extended travel abroad. He was exhausted and collapsed into bed.

Soon after, a light shone in the corner near the door and moved along the floor. It stopped and travelled along the bed and slowly rose up to the duvet. The light flashed across Mr Tarlington's eyes, and then edged along the floor and down the corridor to the lounge. It then continued over to the sound and movie system sat against the wall.

There was a click, and then a flame, followed by a whooshing sound as the flex towards the back of the system caught fire.

The flames gathered momentum, reaching over four feet high, as thick, acrid smoke filled the room before travelling down the corridor towards where Mr Tarlington was sleeping.

As quickly as it had appeared, the torchlight disappeared through a door to the balcony.

The fire took hold within minutes, and the fire alarm in the building sounded.

Mrs Spelter was standing outside in a pink dressing gown as a shadowy figure ran down the metal fire escape away from her flat. She wailed and blew a kiss to the figure disappearing in the direction of the council estate. "Of all the nights," she cursed.

Althea and Seb hugged each other as they stood in the street.

Mr Hamilton hobbled out on a stick with Sabrina and Freya clutching their toys.

Ms Gladstone-Davies rushed to Mr Santiago's and helped him into the evacuation chair with the aid of two fire officers. "I think he needs oxygen," she fussed when Mr Santiago began coughing violently.

"He'll have to be intubated."

A paramedic and a doctor assisted Mr Santiago; Ms Gladstone-Davies clutched his hand.

Mr Tarlington wasn't so lucky. He was later identified by the titanium dental implants found amongst the charred remains in his flat.

The area commander decided to have officers stationed around the clock.

A forensic psychologist was brought in to provide the police with an offender profile. A small, overweight man with thick brown hair and a receding chin stood at the front of a room full of seated police officers. He adjusted his laptop and used a clicker to present his slides.

"He is a loner; someone who finds it difficult to form social ties. He will attempt many types of employment, which don't last longer than a couple of weeks due to a low boredom threshold and his oppositional defiance to following orders." He paused as the slides skipped out of order. "He shows a strong tendency for sadomasochism and perhaps has a gender identity issue."

"So, in a nutshell, who are we looking for?" asked the area commander.

The overweight man skipped to the last slide. "Basically, a psychopath."

The officers looked at each other. But who fitted the description?

The area commander stood up. "Rescreen offenders in the area and look at all the occupants in the area. I need a result ASAP. I want this bastard." He walked over to a transparent Perspex incident board and circled a finger around number three St Swithin's and Seb Zehub. "My money is on him, although number five is a strong possibility." He moved his finger to Mr Hamilton.

"But surely no man would inflict such injuries on himself?" one of the police officers queried.

"The psychologist mentioned sadomasochism. He probably got a kick out of it," the area commander replied, pacing the floor. "I want round-the-clock surveillance, and concealed cameras and listening devices installed. I don't want anyone to know we have St Swithin's fitted out top to bottom with surveillance technology." He lowered his voice and pointed. "And I mean no one. We are laying down a trap." He punched the air as he left.

The police targeted all the occupants of St Swithin's. A van from one of the main utility companies parked across the street. Two officers sat, one monitoring the CCTV, which had been placed near the two properties, number three and number five, and the other listening to devices placed on the exterior walls of all the properties.

They gathered intelligence on the school runs, homework and the latest updates from celebrity shows from number five. In respect of number three, they heard Althea vomit, Seb fart and discussions around who was responsible.

One of the officers laughed. "Number three thinks it's number nine. Oh, and number five thinks it's number one."

"She gives me the creeps, Daddy." The two girls were convinced that Mrs Spelter was the culprit. "And she told us to sod off when we went trick or treating didn't she, Freya? She's a miserable old bag and she has late-night visitors."

Ms Gladstone-Davies at number nine heard something which made her stir. She went into the lounge, switched on the light and saw a shadow cut across the wall into the hallway and out onto the balcony. She was a resourceful woman and knew she'd caught the intruder before he'd caused any damage. She'd lay a trap and set about gathering her tools.

She bought a special substance that showed up under UV light, having seen it used in many crime programmes, which was readily available. She applied the substance around the doorway of the balcony door. Her balcony could only be accessed by two points, so she sprayed the liquid in those areas, too. Any person crossing it would have the substance rubbed onto them and would leave a trace as they left, which she could follow with the aid of the UV light.

She contemplated about telling the police, but she hadn't seen much evidence of detective work; and they'd only send some officer round, which would be common knowledge around the apartments within an hour. No, she would catch whoever was causing the disturbance at St Swithin's.

Ms Gladstone-Davies had gone to visit her sister for the weekend. When she returned, there was a huge pentagon shape daubed in black paint with two garden gnomes buggering each other. She was half expecting something louche to happen and decided to clear it up later. But first she'd shine the UV lamp to see if the visitor had left his calling card.

Waving the light, she saw marks leading along the dining room, out to the balcony and up to the top floor. She unlocked the catch that led to the fire escape up there, climbed onto Mr Santiago's balcony and peered through the window. It was open, so she crept in. She thought about announcing her presence, but didn't want to alert the intruder thinking that Mr Santiago was in danger.

She crept along to a light coming from Mr Santiago's study. She ducked as she tiptoed towards the door and stood crouched near the doorway. The door was ajar. Very slowly, she gave it a little push and it swung open. Hearing laughter, she slowly poked her head towards the direction of the sound.

"You're so good. You clever boy."

Ms Gladstone-Davies's jaw dropped as she saw Mr Santiago sitting in a chair with a homunculus on his lap looking up at its master. The floorboard creaked and the creature turned to face her. She let out a guttural scream. He had the face and body of Mr Santiago, and even wore the same style of clothes.

"My dear, you've discovered my little secret." He sat stroking the miniature-sized version of himself.

"Henri, it's disgusting!" She stood in horror. "But how, why and…?" She stood frozen to the spot. The homunculus sneered at her.

"Because I can. This little fella…" He paused as he stroked its head. "Let's just say I acquired it from a mystic out in Mexico. I had to sell part of my soul, and I thought mobility was neither here nor there, and so he was born." He continued to pet the monstrosity.

Ms Gladstone-Davies slowly moved backwards, but Mr Santiago immediately shifted his gaze to her.

"I wouldn't do that, my dear. Of course, it's most unfortunate you coming in and finding us…"

But before he could finish, she ran towards the balcony.

The homunculus leapt off Mr Santiago's lap and moved swiftly across the floor. Before she could reach the balcony, she felt a searing pain on her calf. She screamed as she looked down. The homunculus had clung to her leg, its jagged teeth ripping into her flesh. She kicked at it, but its grip grew stronger as it began to climb up her.

She dragged herself onto the balcony but before she could scream, the homunculus climbed up onto her back, gripped her around the neck and sank his teeth into her throat.

Her limp body pitched forward as the homunculus let go. She fell over the balcony, her body hitting the pavement below.

The police couldn't rule out whether Ms Gladstone-Davies had committed suicide or if she was a victim of the St Swithin's disturbance.

"Too much of a coincidence and the marks on her neck," one of the police officers said while examining the post-mortem report. "Or maybe she was the perpetrator."

Whether it was a coincidence or not, the disturbances stopped at St Swithin's after Ms Gladstone-Davies's death.

Mrs Spelter decided to sell up and move. "I can't live here anymore." She went to live in Dorset.

Mr Hamilton found a new woman and thought it a good idea to move, too, so the family moved to a quaint village in Leicestershire.

Mr Santiago had a stroke and died, and his executors were in the process of selling his flat, which was still full of all the treasures acquired from his overseas travels, including a large trunk with holes drilled into both sides.

Althea was admitted to hospital, exhausted after giving birth by caesarean. It was touch and go.

Seb sat holding her hand. "He's beautiful. He has your complexion and my hair." He smiled as he kissed his wife.

She drifted off to sleep murmuring.

"You're gorgeous, aren't you?" Seb said, looking at his baby.

The baby opened his eyes, and it was then that he noticed his son had a blown pupil in his right eye.

The Hex

It all started on a gloomy Monday afternoon in October.

You know the type of day, it's dark, cold, wet, and you think to yourself about how you're going to get through the rest of the week. I'd been so tired lately. I was having trouble sleeping, and I couldn't seem to put one foot in front of the other. Wearily, I looked straight ahead at people walking towards me and the pained expressions on their faces as they weaved in and out of each other without registering. Tomorrow it would be repeated again ad infinitum until retirement or death, whichever was soonest.

As I continued to walk further up the street, the droves thinned out. I turned back watching the queues at the bus stop and the entrance to the Tube. The hands bobbing up and down like ducks riding a rough current as people jostled for a cab. I turned and continued, lost in my own thoughts and as I walked further, I found myself outside a shop. I hadn't noticed it before. It was narrow, perhaps less than four feet wide, and the facade beautifully painted: sage green with purple flowers dangling and exotic birds including hummingbirds, parrots, and a toucan, which I felt was staring at me. I moved closer into the doorway. There was a noticeboard advertising acupuncture, naturopathy, kinesiology, aura reading, dowsing, spiritual healing and earth alchemy. The list went on, but the print size grew smaller. I peered closer, and then heard a voice.

"Please come in."

I looked and saw a small man with a Mediterranean complexion and wide smile standing there. I don't know why, but I didn't protest. I walked over the threshold and as I did, I heard something. No, I didn't hear anything – it was a deathly silence you find in churches or in the catacombs under an ancient site. The silence was overpowering, yet when I looked out, buses and cars were racing up and down the street, but I couldn't hear any of them. He pulled out a chair.

"Please." I didn't say anything and moved across to the seat. "You are worried," he said, nodding.

I touched my forehead. I always find myself doing this when feeling stressed. I became aware of it and moved my hand back towards my lap as I sat down.

"Don't worry, I'm going to help you. My name is Mr Hadiba." He held out his hand. I shook it. It's an automatic thing for men to do.

"Fabian Tressla," I said quickly and apologetically.

He had cool hands and cupped them around mine; closing his eyes. I felt myself sinking deeper into the chair as he gripped more firmly. Normally, I would feel uncomfortable, but I didn't. I can't explain it, but I suppose I felt a release.

"Fabian, you look preoccupied." As he said these words, I felt a surge of chemicals flooding my neural synapses, and then all the words came tumbling out.

"I can't sleep. I haven't slept in months. I wake up screaming. I see a green mist and figures surrounding me and this…" I pulled up my jumper sleeve exposing an angry red rash. It covered my arms, legs and part of my body. I'd tried everything, and the dermatologist had prescribed every steroid cream and pill in his toolkit, but nothing had worked. My purge continued. "My stomach hurts all the time, and I have pains in my joints. I've not spoken to anyone about this. I think I'm going out of my mind. I think

I need to be sectioned." I opened my eyes and looked directly at Mr Hadiba. He shook his head and softened his grasp.

"You are not going out of your mind, my friend. Tell me more. I will make you some tea."

I stretched my legs and moved my neck. The tension had lifted, and I felt relaxed. Mr Hadiba disappeared. I could hear rattling.

"I would like to help, Fabian. Please continue." He came out with a tray holding small blue cups and a pot of tea. He handed me a cup and a biscuit. Mr Hadiba pulled out a footstool and lifted my feet. A tacit understanding passed between us as I began to talk again.

"It must have been…" I looked up at the ceiling trying to pinpoint the exact time "Six years ago. I had just got a new job." I paused at that point. I didn't know whether I ought to give the antecedents to my job. Looking at Mr Hadiba, I knew the answer. I then began to relive my past to a total stranger. "I got into the gear." Mr Hadiba raised an eyebrow. "I mean cocaine. I lost my job, I stole money and I was given a suspended prison sentence. Now I'm clean, I go to group therapy – they helped me a lot, the PENDAs."

I could tell Mr Hadiba was struggling to follow me. He placed his hand on my shoulder. I relaxed more and spoke slowly.

"It's a community-based project led by a secular organisation, and they are Brothers. 'PENDA Brothers'. When I say Brothers, I suppose it's a bit like monks, but they're not Bible-bashers or anything like that, but give guidance to people who have lost their way in life."

Mr Hadiba understood.

"Please continue... 'PENDA'. What does that stand for? It is interesting."

"It stands for People, Evolving, Nourishing, Divination Association. They are a wonderful group, and they have helped me a lot. Brother Anton, Rohmer, Hugo, Mason, Tecwin. I couldn't have got that job without them."

Mr Hadiba listened and smiled as he encouraged me to continue.

"And how long have you been going there?" Mr Hadiba sipped from his cup. That was a good question.

"Must be over five years. My mother knew them, or the organisation – she worked as a treasurer. It has been around for years. They are good people. Non-judgemental. They pick up the social pariahs." I put my head down; I'd divulged too much information. I always looked to the ground when I was embarrassed. "I'm sorry. I've said too much... I must be going."

Mr Hadiba placed his hand on my shoulder. "Please." I sat back down. He poured another cup of tea. "And work, tell me more?" I took another sip and continued.

"I'm in a nice team. There is Charlie, Smir. I have close friends – Taylor and Kris."

He nodded and smiled, responding with utterances at the right moments.

I'm not used to people not talking over me or casting their opinions.

"The nightmares, Fabian, you were talking about, tell me more." I tapped my index finger on the lip of the cup.

"It's been years. I don't know if it's connected with the stress at work but—" I broke off and looked at him. "They weren't nightmares; they felt real. I see figures crowding around me. The pain, things going into my legs, my arms and my feet." I laughed hesitantly. "I think I'm going…" Mr Hadiba looked at me. I felt as if he could read my thoughts. He then smiled.

"I am a simple man. I did not go to university. I see colours and I pick up your vibrations. I can sense things." He pointed. "You see – please watch." He stood up in the middle of the shop and held out his hands. "You see where I reach?" I nodded as he spun his arms around. "This is the auric field. This is your protection." I didn't understand. He took a piece of paper off the counter and drew a circle. "Here, this is the energy around you and if anything crosses it or comes into your auric field, it can disturb you unless you're grounded and protected." I looked at Mr Hadiba.

"What, like magic or voodoo?" I felt uncomfortable, but Mr Hadiba just smiled.

"Please, it's not magic. It's the old ways, that's all." He sat back and sipped more of his tea. "You don't need to worry. Please continue." He sat looking at me attentively.

I didn't know what to think. I had nothing to lose so continued. "The sharp pain and the shadowy figures. It was real. I felt a searing pain as something sharp, a knife, ripped through my thigh. And the redness of my skin. It was torture. They were holding me down. I definitely saw a hand, and I screamed out in agony." I looked at Mr Hadiba and felt he knew what I was talking about.

"Please, how often have you had these feelings?"

"They come every two days." I felt upset. "Sometimes I don't see them for a couple of days, and I think they've gone, but they return." I looked down at the Aubusson rug. My eyes followed the pathways into the various mandalas woven within the tapestry. I could see faces emerge.

"They sound very bad. You must be exhausted." He moved forward and tapped my hand.

"The doc says it's the years of taking the gear, I mean cocaine, and I have neural damage which has caused restless legs." I looked at Mr Hadiba. "I've been ever so good and have been clean now for years." I stared at the mandalas again, and the faces had changed.

"What do you think, Fabian?" Mr Hadiba asked. I just shrugged.

"I think he's right. I must have done some damage. I've read up about it. He's prescribed antidepressants. I didn't want to tell him I don't take them. I don't want to be addicted to something else." I paused and looked down at the faces staring at me from the rug. "It's my name."

"Your name, Fabian?" Mr Hadiba looked at me.

The faces changed again, and I saw other images within the mandalas of the rug. I looked up. "Yes, I hear it being called. When the shadows visit, they call my name. They laugh and taunt me." I looked away, feeling tears roll down my face. He leant over and handed me a box of handkerchiefs. "I'm going mad. I'll end up in one of those nutty places rocking back and forth – I know I will."

Mr Hadiba closed his eyes for a moment. A calmness came over me, and the faces in the mandalas looked so friendly. He then opened his eyes and tapped my hand. "You are not mad, my friend."

"But it's not normal. My friend Taylor says I need stronger meds. He thinks I'm suffering."

Mr Hadiba nodded. "And you, Fabian, what do you think?"

I sighed and blinked as the tears stung my eyes. "I have psychosis," I whispered.

Not saying anything, I felt the coolness of his hand resting on mine, which were hot and clammy. He then moved over to a small table and took out a pad and pen and scribbled down something.

"Your friends and your colleagues, please if you would be so kind and say their names again."

I did as I was asked and went through each of their names. Mr Hadiba jotted them down. He made swift hand movements as he wrote.

"I'm sorry. I've taken up too much of your time." I felt self-conscious; here I was telling everything to a total stranger.

"You are here for a reason, Fabian. And this name-calling, can you tell me a little more please to make sure I have everything?" He nodded as he wrote.

I described the name-calling. "I wear earplugs, but they make no difference; besides, they kept falling out so I switched to headphones, but I can still hear them." I looked up. I didn't know whether to carry on.

"Please continue." Mr Hadiba nodded.

Looking at the faces in the mandalas, I sighed. One of them was crying. "I feel as though I can't go on. I was standing on the Tube platform and I just wanted to…" I broke off. I'd disclosed too much. I was offloading to a complete stranger. "I'm sorry. I don't want to outstay my welcome. How much do I owe you?" I got my wallet out. I had thirty pounds. Perhaps I could haggle him down to twenty as I wanted a takeaway on the way home.

"Please, I accept no money." He ushered me to put my wallet back in my jacket pocket. "I've been waiting." He smiled.

"Waiting?" I asked, frowning.

He nodded. "Yes, I knew I had to see someone today who needed my assistance." He stopped writing.

"Are you a counsellor?"

Laughing, he replied, "You don't need counselling, my friend. It is very simple what is at the root of your problem." I looked down at the faces of the mandalas. They appeared to lean forward listening.

"It's in my head." I looked up. "I'm sorry… I must go…"

"Please, you are too harsh on yourself, my friend. These problems of yours, they have a link." I listened as he went on. "You, my dear friend, are hexed. Someone has put a hex on you."

I laughed. "A hex!" Standing up, I said, "I don't believe in that kind of spooky stuff. It's lots of things of my own doing… and …"

"It is a big business, my friend." Mr Hadiba laughed.

"I'm sorry, I don't believe in these things…" I shook my head. "It's just bad luck and bad habits… and …" I walked to the door, but I just froze.

"What you're describing is tormenting your soul. You have a curse and until it's removed, it will keep haunting you," Mr Hadiba said calmly.

"A curse?" I stood glued to the spot. "No, this is too much for me. It is doing my head in. I'm tired. Yes, it's extreme tiredness; it's a sickening mind." I looked around. Everything was neat and orderly and reminded me of an old chemist. There were large glass jars containing liquids of various colours. I didn't remember seeing them before.

"Please, Fabian, sit down. People think curses and hexes are things from bygone years." Mr Hadiba continued to talk. "It is big business. Hexes are handed down from generation to generation." He shook his head before adding, "Believe me, Fabian, they are responsible for many ills of man. They are very powerful." I looked at him. He was so calm and matter-of-fact. I sat back down.

"But why…? Why would anyone want to hex me? Is it because of what I've done in the past? I'm a bad person, is that what you're saying?" I looked at him, but he just smiled. I was finding this whole conversation incredible. Here I was talking to a complete stranger about my troubles, and he was putting it down to a hex. I remembered going to the drugs counsellor who'd said I needed to take responsibility for my own actions. Surely blaming a hex wasn't taking that responsibility? I was confused.

"Please, I can see this is causing you much disbelief, but a hex will stay with the person until it is removed, or…" He looked and nodded. "It is very bad if it stays around. The person will be in the torment, and if it isn't removed…" He broke his gaze and looked away.

I felt really hot. I couldn't quite register what he was saying. "You mean until I'm dead or killed?" Mr Hadiba nodded. I looked down at the mandalas within the rug; they all nodded, too. "Surely… if I do have a hex, how do I go about having it removed?"

"That, my dear friend, is where I come in." Mr Hadiba opened his arms. "You see, I have been very interested in what you've told me. "I've made notes and written down the names of the people." He moved back over to the counter. " But, I need a complete list of places you have lived and worked, even if you were only there for a short time." He gathered up the cups. "I will make you some more tea, and you sit there and close your eyes. It will be easier to remember."

I did as he said and as I closed my eyes, I felt so relaxed. I could hear whispering. Listening, all the names and places came to me with such ease, as though someone was delving into the deep recesses of my mind. I must have regressed quite deeply because when I opened my eyes, Mr Hadiba was standing over me holding a cup of tea. I looked down and saw names and places scribbled on pieces of paper.

"I don't…" I started.

"You see, it is easy when you relax," he said, handing me the tea.

"But what now?"

Mr Hadiba looked at the pieces of paper. "I would like you to think of someone who may have ill feelings against you."

"That could be quite a list." I laughed. "I mean I've pissed off so many people in my time…" I felt my cheeks burn. "I'm sorry, I mean I've upset quite a few, and then there's the cheating and dumping of previous girlfriends."

"Try to remember."

"But…" I looked at him and laughed again. "Perhaps there was a committee of hatred," I suggested. I started to run off a few names. "Ginny, yes she hated me. Maisie, Bron and Kathy. Then there was Nigel when I went off with Sandy." I sank into the chair. "I've been a total bastard, and now my past is catching up with me." I looked at Mr Hadiba, who was writing down the names. "This is karma." Mr Hadiba ignored me as he continued to scribble away as I rolled off more names. I stopped. I couldn't think of any more.

"I would like you to put the names of your closest friends each on a piece of paper." Mr Hadiba handed me the pad. I did what I was told and then handed them back to him. He gathered all the pieces of paper together. "You will have to fold each one and say the following, 'Go back bad deed to the one who deed you. Take back bad deed to that who did deed you.'"

I felt such an idiot, but I did as I was instructed and placed all the folded pieces of paper into the box. He then closed the lid.

"I'll put it in a safe place." He placed the box on the counter.

"How will I know when…?" I pointed to the box. "That it's worked…?" I walked over to the counter. Mr Hadiba ushered me to the door. He was obviously getting bored of me. "But your fee… I must pay you."

"Please, we can settle up later." He put his hand on mine.

The next thing I knew, I was sitting on the Tube looking out of the window watching as we rumbled through the stations. I rubbed my eyes. I think I'd been daydreaming and looked around to see that the carriage was empty. Perhaps I had imagined Mr Hadiba.

"Fabian, Fabian, Fabian."

My eyes opened as I heard my name being repeated again and again. I looked at the clock on my bedside cabinet. It was three in the morning. My eyes closed and then, "Fabian, Fabian, Fabian."

All night, my eyes opened and closed at the repetition of my name, and then I felt something. I felt a pressure on my arms and legs. Dear God, I was being held down as something sharp seared through my abdomen.

I woke up screaming, my hands clutching my stomach. I jumped out of bed and cowered in the corner.

"Leave me alone!" I screamed. I must have sat there for hours. Then I was cold, and crawled back into bed to go to sleep.

As my eyes closed again, I saw figures circling me. My body was burning; the rash more painful and redder.

When I finally awoke, I felt so weak and exhausted that I couldn't even think straight. I had even forgotten how to switch on the kettle. I went to the fridge to look for teabags, but ended up putting gravy granules in my mug. Everything was wrong; I couldn't figure it out.

I was going to call in sick for work, but I couldn't. I had already been given a warning for taking time off, so it would go against me. I looked in the mirror and saw the dark circles and the rash around my neck. I dragged my body down the street. The effort to consciously put one foot in front of the other was unbearable and my head was so heavy. It was worse than any bender I'd been on.

The voices around me intensified. I winced in pain as I held my hands to my ears. I then caught my reflection in the Tube window. I looked like Edvard Munch's *The Scream*. I was maxed-out on painkillers and put my head down. I just didn't want to talk to anyone. I had to see Mr Hadiba... But did he exist? I just wasn't sure.

I don't know how I managed to get through the day. All I remember is being shoved and pushed as I headed up the street and as I looked up, I saw Mr Hadiba standing in his doorway. He'd changed and was wearing a green waistcoat.

"My friend, please come in. I'll make us some tea." He ushered me inside.

I wanted to punch him. I must have lost it at that point, as I started screaming and shouting and accusing him of all sorts – witchcraft, voodoo – and he just stood there while I continued my outburst. He ushered me to a chair. I refused at first, but felt so tired that I sat down as he made me coffee. It was strong.

He handed me a plate of food. They were small cakes in cubes. As I ate one, I could taste spices, herbs and something else. I felt calmer and the mandalas in the rug looked up smiling. I looked at Mr Hadiba and apologised. I felt embarrassed by my behaviour.

"Fabian, tell me about what has happened."

I relived the terror of last night and how everything seemed worse. Louder and longer, the name-calling and the pains. Mr Hadiba nodded. "The box, Mr Hadiba." I ate another of the cakes. "The hex... The names... It didn't work." I finished off the last of the cakes. I felt so relaxed.

"It's simple, my friend, and easily remedied." He smiled.

"Simple? I was petrified last night. I thought I was going to die, and you say it's simple." I felt my heart racing again.

"I am sorry. I mean the people on the list in the box are not the ones responsible for your hex."

I sighed heavily. I didn't know why I'd come back. "How do you know?" I felt irritated.

"It is trial and error to begin with, but you will know when the hex is lifted." He walked over to the counter and got a pad and handed to me. "I would like you to write the names of everyone you can think of." He looked at me. "All the people, no matter how insignificant they have been."

I did as I was asked as Mr Hadiba poured me another cup of coffee. I looked around thinking of other names, and then down at the mandalas. Faces emerged and I could see names being called out. I wrote frantically. I folded the pages I'd scribbled on and placed them in the box.

"Please, clear your mind and repeat after me, 'Go back bad deed to the one who deed you. Take back bad deed to that who did deed you.'"

I repeated after him, but stumbled on the second line. "...to that who did deed you," I said slowly.

Mr Hadiba helped by repeating the last words to me. "I promise you, my friend," he said smiling, "you will have a most beautiful sleep." He took my hand and cupped it. "Your problems will be gone. Trust me. Now, you go." He ushered me out of the shop.

"But I need to pay you." I took out my wallet. "Do you take cards? I have some cash. Here, forty pounds, please take it."

He pushed the cash back into my hand. "You can settle later..." He smiled. "I want you to do a good deed on the way home. It is very important to do a good deed."

I looked at him and frowned. "But I don't understand. The last time you..."

Mr Hadiba nodded. "It is different, my friend. You must trust me. You need to do a good deed; you will know when it is done." He accompanied me out of the shop. "Please remember to do a good deed – it is important," he repeated as he stood in the doorway.

"A good deed… and I'll know when it's done," I repeated to myself.

I looked for situations in which I could do a good deed. I rushed to open the door for an elderly lady, but someone got there before me. I was about to give up my seat to a woman with a pushchair on the Tube, but a middle-aged woman beat me to it. I was going to slip the forty pounds into the hat of a busker, but he packed up and hailed a cab. I couldn't find any opportunity of doing a good deed.

Then a man's wallet fell out of his back pocket. I rushed over to grab it when a voice shouted, "Mister, your wallet." The old man turned, saw me go for it and scowled.

I'll find something tomorrow – something big to do. I'll buy dinner for Kris. I've been ignoring him lately… I can phone the numbers in my little black book. I smiled. *Yes, I will do that – apologise for being a bastard and allow them to vent. That will be my good deed. Mr Hadiba said I will know.*

I crossed the road and heard singing. I walked along rehearsing what I'd say to each of them: "I've seen the error of my ways." That sounded too insincere. I looked up and saw the lights at the PENDA Community Centre. I hadn't been there for a few weeks. I walked down the pathway and could smell something good.

"Hello, Fabian, it's lovely to see you," a voice announced from under a mop of red hair. Brother Tecwin was tuning his guitar as he sat on a high stool in the porch. He strung a few chords. "How does it sound?"

"Bang on the money."

I could see the other Brothers loading up one of the trestle tables with all sorts of goodies. Brothers Anton and Hugo were dishing out stew. Brother Rohmer was cutting up huge wedges of crusty bread, and Brother Mason was piping custard into buns.

"Please come in. So nice to see you, Fabian. Sit here." Brother Anton pulled out a chair. He was a cuddly bear type who would do anything for anyone. He helped me take my coat off.

Brother Hugo was the fit one. I often teased him as being a silver fox.

Brother Rohmer was the quiet one. He was a thinker, and I could never really tell what was going on in his head. He was very much the intelligence behind PENDA. He was a good fundraiser, especially in marketing and strategy. While he wasn't loquacious, he had a way about him. He was meticulous and more mindful. I knew little about him. He'd come from a middle-class background. I always sensed that he hadn't lived up to his parents' expectations. But perhaps that was the true value of being a PENDA Brother. All of them had had trauma before entering the brotherhood.

Tecwin was into drugs, mainly crack. Anton's was food and cottaging. He was now a self-proclaimed celibate and would often state, "The only cottaging I do now is what I put in between two pieces of wholemeal bread." Hugo suffered depression and had attempted suicide several times for a variety of reasons. "I was a magnate for bad luck," he'd often said. Brother Mason was a drifter and on the streets for many years. And Brother Rohmer's was theft. He'd lost a prominent position as an accountant and served a long prison sentence for fraud.

They all now seemed content and happy having found an inner peace.

"Brother Fabian." Brother Mason cleared his throat. "We were thinking it was time you joined us. You have all the necessary skills and commitment, and you'd save a fortune if you moved in."

They all looked down the table at me. I was gobsmacked. They were all kind and always there for me. I felt I belonged.

Brother Mason leant forward. "Do I sense the cogs are turning in our favour, Brother?" I nodded as I pondered.

"Perhaps." I looked across at them. "But I haven't been here for ages and… I feel…" I continued to eat as the Brothers looked at me. "I'd have to… It's a huge undertaking, and besides… I'd have to give notice at work and also on my flat." I looked at Brother Mason. "What happens if it doesn't work out? I'll be homeless as well as jobless."

Brother Anton smiled. "That isn't going to happen. You, sir, have a calling."

I looked at them all and felt this inner peace travel through my body. As I nodded, I could hear Mr Hadiba's voice. I smiled. "Okay, I'll join."

Brother Anton clapped. "It's time for a celebration. I have mead. Brother Tecwin, the amber nectar and some glasses. The senate will be happy to see a new Brother. We are all going tomorrow. Perhaps Brother Fabian will be coming, too."

"Yes, of course I'll come." I felt so happy. "Besides, I'm resigning, so I'll call in sick." I gave my solid undertaking to arrive at the PENDA Community Centre by eleven o'clock the next morning to start my journey. A journey I knew was right for me.

But that night my stomach was performing somersaults; I rushed back and forth to the bathroom. At one point, I fell asleep on the toilet not having the strength to move. I crawled into bed at around four in the morning. My alarm went off at nine o'clock. I called into work describing my symptoms. But the truth was that I did feel like shit. My guts were in torment, and I curled up with a hot water bottle. I also phoned Brother Anton.

"Brother, I'm so ill. I won't be able to make it, but I'll still be joining you, so please tell the senate. I can email you to confirm."

Brother Anton said he'd have my room ready and that I could move my stuff in next week. "Speedy recovery, Fabian, and Vivian, our devoted treasury and administrator, will be in contact to arrange for your things to be brought over. No time like the present."

I drifted in and out of sleep all that day. I hadn't experienced such a deep sleep in years. It felt as if each muscle was getting an intense massage. When I drifted deeper, I felt something lift. It's difficult to describe, but I could see something move away from me, and then I heard a deep groan. It was so loud that I remember opening my eyes and looking around. No one was there, but I had this overwhelming feeling that life was good.

Stretching each muscle I felt so relaxed. I looked at the clock to see that it was two in the afternoon. I sat up. I'd go into town as I needed to tell Mr Hadiba.

I sat on the Tube looking at the people around me. I felt a sense of peace. Everyone looked happy; I felt happy and I punched the air as I walked up the street to see Mr Hadiba.

I must pay him, I thought to myself. I continued walking and humming to myself. I felt so happy. I reached where I thought the shop was and looked. I couldn't see it. I went into a newspaper shop nearby.

"Please, a shop…" I didn't know how to describe it. "A health shop, a pharmacy… A Mr Hadiba? Do you know where it is?" The woman looked at me and shook her head.

"No, I'm sorry, I'm new. I'll ask my boss." An older man was stacking shelves. He'd heard the conversation.

"I can't think of a shop. You say pharmacy. There used to be one. Closed years ago."

"Are you sure? It was next door."

The man shook his head. "Sorry, it's been closed for years. He died or something."

"I must have the wrong area. I'll look further up the street." I walked out and stood back looking at the shops. "It was along here – I'm sure of it," I said to myself before continuing to walk, but I couldn't find it. Deciding to go into a pub, I bought a pint and sat in the corner. It was surprisingly empty.

As I drank, I looked at the TV screen which dominated one side of the wall. The sound was off, but the subtitles were on. I got up to buy another drink.

"Sorry, mate, I need to change the barrel."

I stood watching the news. A man cheered as the fruit machine began flashing and making whooping noises. He was happy he'd won the jackpot. I looked up at the TV again. It was the usual things about politics, and then a breaking news banner appeared at the bottom of the screen.

Moving closer, I read the subtitles as the newscaster announced, *"…a minibus crash on the M1.*

The minibus contained the Brothers from the PENDA Society. They were all pronounced dead at the scene. Their vehicle collided with two other cars – one carrying five men returning from a football match and the other... a young couple who had just announced their engagement... From emergency service eyewitness accounts, it has been described as one of the worst crashes for decades. The reason for the crash is unknown, although witnesses describe seeing an elderly man with a Mediterranean complexion wearing a green waistcoat standing at the central reservation. One witness reported him walking into the path of the PENDA's minibus, but his body is yet to be recovered..."

Jet

Cats use clever psychology to call birds down pretending to be their friends and playing, rolling around exposing their fluffy bellies. But their softness changes and their claws emerge serrating and decapitating. They use the same subtle techniques to entrap new owners with their party tricks of lifting a paw and meowing, especially when sitting on a windowsill drenched.

"It's no good. I can't bear it any longer." Anna flung open back door and in trotted Jet purring with her tail up.

She soon nestled into the matrimonial bed, where Geoff would sleep diagonally in order to avoid waking her. Jet had a distinguished lineage as she had impeccable manners and was more humanlike.

"There are days when I swear I see a face," Anna would say as she looked across at the cat sleeping. No one quite knew where Jet had come from or her age. She had appeared at Geoff and Anna's housing association flat more than ten years ago when food kept going missing. First a haddock left defrosting on a worktop in the kitchen with the door ajar. Next was the chicken that Geoff swore was on the kitchen table. And then a big pot of minced beef. The mystery was only solved when Anna came in one day and saw a sleek black coat disappear through the half-open window. It was her colour and stealthy behaviour that earnt the cat her name.

"Jet," Geoff said. Anna looked at him and nodded.

"She's obviously been used to the better things in life. She will not sleep on anything which isn't made of good quality wool or fabric. And she'll not eat tinned food. I'm sure she makes herself vomit on purpose in order to get steak and chicken." Anna blew out her cheeks as she lightly pan-fried an out-of-date steak.

Jet sat with her paw raised in anticipation watching Anna finely chop up the steak. The cat surveyed the bowl inspecting the quality of the meat, turned up her nose and walked over to the litter tray, stepped in with her back paws and tossed all the litter out across the kitchen floor before majestically walking through the back door.

"Well, I'll be…!" Anna tossed Jet's food in the bin and took out another piece of steak reserved for Geoff. Jet soon returned weaving her body in between Anna's legs as she placed the cat's meat in evenly cut cubes.

"All in your head, love," Geoff would say as he carried on watching TV. "We will just have to be careful because we're not allowed pets. If the cronies across the way find out, it's curtains." Geoff crossed his hands on his chest. "Mourn the loss."

Anna threw a magazine at him. "She's had your steak, so I'd start doing overtime if I were you. Besides, they don't bother about cats; it's dogs they object to." Anna nestled down on the sofa.

Jet placed her two paws on the edge of the armrest. Anna sighed as she moved along. Geoff did the same as Jet took over one side of the sofa with the couple now hemmed in on the other side.

"She's so demanding. Worse than any teenager," Geoff said trying to retrieve the TV magazine from under Anna's bottom.

"You were saying?" Anna looked at Geoff, who was looking at Jet, outstretched, her back paws digging into his wife's back.

"Do you think we should buy a three-seater?" Geoff looked at Anna, who then looked back at Jet.

Jet looked up and meowed before cleaning her face.

"The boss said 'yes'." Anna laughed.

Geoff flicked through the channels as Anna sat attempting a tricky sudoku.

"Oh no! I've repeated number six twice." She tossed the magazine on the floor, causing Jet to stir.

"Shush, love, you've woken her."

Anna got up and curtsied. "I'm so sorry, Mistress Jet." She watched the cat look up and for a brief moment, she saw a smile. "I swear she's human. You know black cats are supposed to be familiars associated with witches or lost souls."

"It's a cat," said Geoff, before changing the channel again. "She must have been used to one of those spacious houses in Bury Mead Lane. Parquet floors, a kitchen the size of a football pitch and lovely mullion windows, climbing roses and landscaped gardens."

Anna stroked Jet, who purred and began licking her. "She's probably been bought for a son of an architect. No, a surgeon famous for pioneering work."

Geoff looked over and rolled his eyes. "She got short-changed. Look where she's ended up. With two old farts." Anna hit her husband's arm.

"You're so rude. Not in front of the cat." Anna covered her pet's ears. "He's just jealous. You're so beautiful." Jet yawned and extended her back paws, exposing more of her fluffy tummy. "Mummy loves

Jet and her long, gorgeous body." She buried her head into Jet's tummy. The cat looked up, purred and stuck her claws into Anna's head.

Geoff laughed as Jet sat bolt upright rubbing her head against Anna's arm. "You see, you only get so many strokes before you'll have to pay."

Anna rubbed her head. "The little devil!" She looked at Jet, who touched her wrist with the soft pad of her paw. She began licking her.

"Jet, chicken!" Geoff called.

The cat immediately shot off the sofa in the direction of the kitchen.

"It really is like having an adolescent daughter," said Anna.

Jet spent most of her days lolling in the warmest parts of the flat. Invariably, this meant she had to move every couple of hours to follow the sun. When she did venture out, she'd cross over to number twenty-four, another ground-floor flat, which was owned by Denys Smyth. He was once a man of means who had fallen on hard times and spent the majority of his time in the garden. He'd worked on a new vegetable patch, raking the soil over, planting seeds and placing rows of string in lines. Jet pawed along the soil and sat looking around smiling as she did a huge dump. She sniffed it and attempted to cover it, but lost interest and strolled off, her tail swaying high.

"You little sod!" Denys ran out with a spray bottle. Jet turned and hissed refusing to move. In revenge, Denys lobbed a stone at her. Jet dived under a bush. Mr Smyth raked over the vegetable patch again and brought out his deckchair and radio and had a snooze.

Walking along and into his kitchen, Jet helped herself to a pork chop he'd left out to cook later. She pulled bags out of one of his cupboards, and then went back over to his vegetable patch to urinate before picking up the chop and running off.

"Why, you little...!" Mr Smyth ran after her shouting, throwing stones and spraying water.

Jet jumped up on the ledge and when he approached her, she spat and scratched his arm, drawing blood. She then retreated and trotted back in the direction of Anna and Geoff's.

A letter written in red pen was posted through Anna and Geoff's letterbox. Anna read out the letter to her husband.

" *'Get rid of the cat or I will, signed Anon.'* Who do you think it's from?" Anna stood looking out of the lounge window. "Perhaps we can get more litter trays, or don't feed her such rich foods or those specialist dry foods, then she won't go using all the neighbours' gardens as toilets," she suggested.

"We could try, love. I don't want to lose her," said Geoff, looking down as Jet weaved in between his legs before jumping onto his shoulder.

"Right, Messy Missy, no more annoying neighbours, you understand?" Jet brushed her face against Geoff's. He could feel tears welling up.

"She understands so much," Anna said, and then looked over to Denys Smyth's house. "There's something odd about him. Wasn't he one of those presenters on a TV show in the 1980s?" She watched him watering his garden. "That's all he does. Water his bloody garden and get drunk."

Anna placed an array of biscuits she'd bought from the pet shop on the kitchen table.

"This one is for house cats… This for mature ones." She looked at Jet, who turned her head in disgust. "This one is for sensitive tummies… This is for sensitive mouths… Oh, this one is for urinary tract problems, and this one is for sensitive skin."

Geoff looked at the receipt. "You must have spent over fifty pounds."

"She's worth it." Jet jumped up and brushed against Geoff.

"Okay, I get it, all this attention from you girls," he teased.

Anna laughed as Jet jumped onto Geoff's shoulder.

She purred by his ear, and for a moment he thought he could hear a girl's voice. He looked at Jet, who then brushed her face against his.

Jet appeared to toe the line as Anna and Geoff set down the ground rules. She knew if she behaved, she'd be rewarded. Friday night was the highlight of the week for the household. Anna and Geoff would settle down on the sofa with huge bucket of chicken, Jet sitting in between purring loudly with her little paper plate resting on a serviette.

"Your Friday night treat," said Anna before topping up Jet's plate.

Jet gobbled it up, and then purred at Geoff.

When Anna wasn't looking, Geoff would top up Jet's plate as well. Anna pretended not to notice. She knew Geoff loved the cat, and that was what was important.

They were a family snuggling up each evening. Anna and Geoff squeezed together with Jet lying prostrate over a memory cushion that moulded around her body.

The winter was now drawing in. "We can't let her get cold during the day," Anna said looking at Jet curled up on the sofa. "We're going to have to put the heating on. She can't generate heat like she used to." Geoff knew he'd have to relent because Anna was right.

Jet was having trouble getting onto the bed, so he would often lift her up. She also had one or two accidents; neither of them made a fuss. Jet became more lethargic, and Geoff would coax her out to get some fresh air and maybe eat a little grass. She would poke her head out, but wandered slowly back inside to the warmth. Jet's appetite began to lessen, and Geoff noticed vomit on the lounge floor; as he bent down to clean it up, he noticed specks of blood. He'd also noticed blood when cleaning out the litter tray. Jet was sleeping more.

"It wouldn't surprise me if she's being poisoned." Anna looked across at Denys ambulating around his garden drunk. He looked up and stared at her.

The next day, Anna and Geoff took their beloved cat to see Mr Fontana, the vet.

"She needs surgery, or else I cannot guarantee…" Mr Fontana felt Jet's tummy and gently prodded the large growth.

Jet hissed and scratched the vet's hand. Geoff had never heard Jet make such a noise before. He wiped away his tears while the vet continued his assessment.

"Is it cancerous?" asked Geoff as Mr Fontana helped him place Jet into the cage. Anna took her out to the waiting room before the vet ushered Geoff over.

"If it's cancer, she has a fifty per cent chance…"

Geoff went out to the waiting room and put his arm around Anna. "Let's get this little beauty home, and it's sirloin steak tonight."

Jet purred.

"It's not good, is it, love?" Anna burst into tears as Geoff drove back home.

Geoff shook his head. "Bloody pets, why do they get to you?"

Anna looked at Jet sitting in the basket on her lap. "We'll get through this." She poked her fingers into the cage and the cat licked them and purred.

When they got home, Anna and Geoff discussed whether it was fair on Jet to put her through surgery. They weighed up the options.

"It's four thousand pounds, Anna. We don't have the money, and the vet has only given her a fifty-fifty chance of surviving. The costs will increase if it is cancer, as the chemotherapy costs will be another two to three thousand." Geoff looked through their bank and credit card statements.

"We can cancel the cruise for our silver wedding anniversary. We can get back the deposit," Anna said as she hurried into the bedroom. She came back holding something in her hand. "I can sell this." She held up an eighteen-carat gold bracelet.

"I can't let you sell that, love. Your dad gave you that," Geoff said, shaking his head.

Anna pushed it into his hands. "It's no good to me, and he'd understand." She looked across at a photograph of her father in his military uniform. It was the last photo taken of him.

Geoff sat up all night looking through the policies they both held, savings, premium bonds, and items they could sell. He scribbled down figures as Anna brought him a mug of tea.

"We could get a loan or sell the car. We can get an older one," Anna suggested.

"What, to add to all the other loans? Remember the debts we took on for the business venture with your cousin." Geoff looked up. "I'm sorry, love, I didn't mean that. It was just as much my fault." He punched numbers into the calculator. "I could sell my watch and I'm sure we'll find other things we could sell." He looked around the lounge.

"It's not fair." Anna burst into tears. "We've helped so many people in our lives and look at us. We're in our early fifties, yet we can't even afford a bloody vet's bill! It's all so hopeless."

Geoff stopped using the calculator and hugged his wife. "Shush, don't worry, love. We'll raise the money."

"I just feel such a failure. Bloody cousin Sally's crappy business venture and us losing our house over it – now look at us. Living in a dosshouse!" Anna screamed. "I can't stand it!" She looked at Jet, who was asleep on the sofa, her breathing laboured. "And our poor…" Anna knelt down next to the sofa crying.

Jet looked up, blinked and sat up. She wobbled as she jumped off the sofa and limped towards Anna.

Anna looked down at her. "I can't bear this. It's breaking my heart, Geoff. Just get the money any way we can. Take any loans out – it's just money," she wept. The cat sat looking at them both and purred.

Jet had the surgery and recovered much quicker than expected. She waited to be collected as she sat on a blanket peering out of a cage at the vets.

"There she is," said Anna, cooing. "She looks so well." She went over to Jet.

With a forced smile, Mr Fontana pulled Geoff to one side. "I'm sorry. It is cancer, and the growth is more extensive than anticipated. It has spread to her lungs. We can start chemotherapy, but given her age it would not extend her life."

Geoff stared down at the floor. "I see. How long has she got?"

The vet looked at Anna. "With the love and support of your wife and yourself, I would say four months. She's strong, but if her breathing gets more laboured, I would recommend euthanasia. It is the kindest thing you can do. See how you go. I can give you painkillers which should help over the next few weeks." Mr Fontana handed him a bottle of tablets.

"How will I know when it's time?" asked Geoff, tears stinging his eyes.

"You'll know when it's time to let her go."

Walking slowly over to Anna, Geoff wiped his eyes. "Look, she's licking."

Anna looked at Geoff and smiled. "She's coming home, aren't you, Jet?"

Jet licked Geoff's hand when he put it out to her.

"Yes, love. Jet is coming home." He squatted down and tickled the cat under her chin. She meowed and purred. Anna rested her head on her husband's shoulder.

Geoff made a ladder, which Anna covered with carpet so Jet could get onto the sofa more easily. He also made a little cot that had a heat pad. They moved the litter trays so she had less distance to travel, but Geoff started to become more distant.

At first, Anna put it down to stresses at work. He had recently been made supervisor, and there were staffing problems – the usual employee issues of absenteeism and apathy due to management change and restructuring. But he had also become more irritable, moodier and withdrawn.

"What's got into you? I say good morning, and you snap my head off!" Anna slammed down her mug.

"It's just work and things." Geoff shrugged and avoided her gaze.

It was on a Thursday night when Anna discovered letters from the housing association demanding payment of over one thousand pounds within seven days, otherwise they would issue legal proceedings.

"I don't understand. How come we owe all this money?" Anna asked, thrusting the letters towards Geoff.

"The vet bills. I couldn't raise enough on your jewellery and my watch." He turned away.

Jet sat up watching them argue.

"I thought you got over a thousand for them both."

"I got two hundred for both," replied Geoff, leaning on the table.

"Two hundred?" Anna looked at her husband in disbelief. "My necklace was worth twice as much!" she snapped. "And your watch at least four hundred. Why?"

"I had no choice." Geoff walked over to the window. "We needed the money, but I couldn't raise it quickly enough. The vet needed it within four weeks or else he said the surgery would be hopeless."

He stared out across at the trees standing barren against the winter skyline. Jet meowed.

Anna turned away shaking. She looked at the letters. "We can pay extra surely. I'll call them."

That night, Geoff slept on the sofa, with Jet nestling closely alongside him.

The next morning, Anna could hear voices on the doorstep and someone banging and ringing the doorbell. She flung the door open.

"Stop pressing the bloody bell! I'm not deaf!" Anna barked at two people standing on the doorstep.

"Mrs Meadows, I'm Gina, a housing officer. I have to serve you legal papers." The young woman held out an A4 envelope. Anna froze. The woman continued to push the envelope towards Anna. "I'll put this here." The woman placed it on a ledge near the front door. There was a man standing behind her who Anna recognised.

"We've received complaints about a pet you have. A dog, I'm told."

Anna looked at Councillor Skellington as he pushed his way forward. "It's a cat," she replied, before realising her mistake.

"So, you admit to having a pet? That is forbidden in your tenancy and with the shocking arrears of rent, I expect the housing association will have no difficulty in having you evicted. And not soon enough in my opinion. Your cat has been destroying your neighbour's garden and is probably urinating everywhere. It's disgusting." He stood pointing. Anna watched as he continued his tirade and couldn't help but notice the long grey and black hairs creeping out of his nostrils as they flared.

"Oh, bugger off. You can't bear the fact that we opposed the regeneration scheme. This is a personal vendetta; no court will allow our eviction!" Anna slammed the door, narrowly missing the councillor's nose. She heard him shouting and declaring vengeance.

Geoff stood in the kitchen as Anna flung the envelope onto the kitchen floor and began jumping up and down on it.

"I hate you! I hate you! And I wish you a long, lingering death, you piece of shit!" she screamed.

Anna went upstairs to have a lie down. Geoff opened the envelope. The housing association told them that they had to leave within twenty-eight days.

Geoff phoned them in the morning and arranged for the arrears to be spread over a longer period, but the housing association helpline suggested otherwise.

"I'm sorry, but we have to go to court. It's head office's steer, not my decision you understand. Still, you can get a suspended order if you take all the paperwork, but there is one thing—"

"One thing I don't understand," said Geoff, frowning. "If we make a payment plan, don't you have to rescind court proceedings?" He listened as the man tapped away on the keyboard.

"I just spoken to my supervisor. The cat is going to have to go. You'll also have to decant because the regeneration has been given the green light." The man continued to tap away. "If you agree to those conditions, I'll see if I can contact the court."

"It's a cat." Geoff breathed heavily. "Wait a minute, it's that Councillor Skellington and our opposition to the move. I get it – he wants us out because we wouldn't be decanted the other year. I see… dirty tricks. Well, the cat's not going, and I'll fight you in court." Geoff hung up and kicked the side of the table.

Jet looked up and meowed. She got up and tried to get down from the sofa. Geoff walked over.

"Shush now. Don't tire yourself, Jet. You rest. Everything is all right."

Jet's breathing became more laboured. Geoff increased the painkillers as he sat cuddling her on the sofa. Anna was looking at the new property they'd been offered by the housing association.

"It's on the third floor." She looked at the letter and enclosures and then across at Jet. "Councillor Skellington has won. We have no option but to move, but…" Anna looked at Geoff. He was clinging to Jet.

"I think it will be soon, love."

Anna listened to Jet struggling to breathe. She was no longer cleaning herself and struggled to get to the litter tray. "Should we think about calling the vet?" Anna nestled her head on Geoff's shoulder as he pressed his body warmth around the cat.

That night, all three of them fell asleep on the sofa, the only noise being Jet's breathing.

When Geoff awoke, he thought he saw a young girl standing by the door smiling.

Anna stirred and looked at Geoff and then across at the door to see the little girl disappear through the door. He felt Jet's body. She was cold.

They arranged for Jet to be cremated. Anna wrote a poem and Geoff said a couple of anecdotes as they both took it in turns to sprinkle Jet's ashes. Anna put two rose quartz crystals in the soil and blew a kiss.

"Thank you for coming into our lives again, my sweet darling." Geoff hugged Anna as they both stood silently next to the grave of their baby daughter.

Jasmine Meadows. Born asleep.

The Bus Shelter

A man swayed as he stood on the steps of the nightclub. The bouncer gave him a nudge, which made him stumble down the steps, causing him to hit his head. For a moment, he stared blankly at the night sky.

"Leave him alone, you big bully!" A girl rushed across and bent over the man. "Are you all right?" The man looked up and stared. "You okay?" she repeated. The man continued to stare and blinked looking up at the girl. "Do you have any mates who can help you?" He attempted to sit up but fell backwards. "Can't one of you help?" the girl screamed at the bouncers standing at the entrance. She knelt down and helped the man into a sitting position, placing her hand on the small of his back. "Where are you going?" The man pushed the girl's hand away.

"It's okay, I can do it myself." He rubbed his head and looked at the girl. "Far Cotton. Just past Far Cotton." The man attempted to get up. His mobile phone lay in pieces on the ground. "Shit!" he yelled.

"Do you think you can make it to the wall?"

The man nodded and put his arm over the girl's shoulder. They shuffled to a low wall at the side of the nightclub.

"This place is getting worse. They should be ashamed of themselves!" she shouted in the direction of one the bouncers, who was pacing up and down shouting into a mobile phone. "I've ordered a cab." She looked around. "It should have been here ages ago… If you want, we could split the fare. I'm Mia." She steadied the man against the wall.

"Hey, nice to meet you, Mia. Sam here." He held out his hand.

"You out celebrating?"

Sam nodded, and then looked down at Mia's bare feet and legs covered in scratches.

"Yeah, looks a mess. I…" She searched her handbag. "I don't understand… the cab… My phone, I thought it was in here."

Sam leant against the wall while Mia continued to search through her bag.

There was a loud thunderclap followed by lightning which zigzagged across the night sky. Sam looked up as the rain came down.

"Oh no!" Mia shrieked, the rain now pummelling down on them.

"Come on." He grabbed Mia's hand, and they stumbled towards the direction of the busy interchange.

Mia closed her eyes as Sam led her across the road weaving in and out of the traffic to the taxi rank. There was a long queue. A woman with crimped hair and large looped earrings stared at Mia.

"If we walk further down here—" Sam pointed down a narrow street "—we can probably hail one at the road next to the junction." They clung to each other hobbling down the narrow street.

"I'm getting friggin' soaked! Can we take cover somewhere?" Sam gripped Mia's hand tightly and led her further down the narrow street. "Are you sure this leads anywhere?" she shouted.

Sam pointed. "Over there." He pulled her in the direction of a small, squat building standing on the corner at the bottom of the street. It was a concrete bus shelter with thick, toughened square block glass down one side and a bulkhead light that dimly lit the interior. "We can take cover here." Sam led her into the bus shelter.

"Shit!" Mia shook her hands. "I'm soaked right through... My make-up." She took a mirror out of her handbag. "Look at my eyes." She angled the mirror towards the dull glow of the light at the back of the shelter. "Lifeless." She attempted to muss up her hair. "My face." Sam looked up and laughed. "I don't know why you think it's so funny. Take a look at yourself." She handed him the mirror.

He stared at his flat hair stuck down with hair gel and congealed blood. He felt a huge gash at the back of his head.

"Here, use this." She held out a handkerchief decorated with pink flowers and a large "M" embroidered on it. "A present from my nan – she likes to give me girly things."

"It's stopped bleeding." He waved his hand at her. "The gel has helped," Sam added, trying to look at the gash in the mirror.

"Does it hurt?"

"No, it feels numb." Sam handed back the mirror and sat down on the wooden slatted bench.

"You don't know what's been on there. Look... your trousers."

"It's dry, that's the main thing," he said with a shrug.

Mia looked upwards to the roof of the shelter. "The rain must have stopped. I can't hear anything."

"It's still raining, look!" He pointed at the rain lashing down.

Following his gaze, Mia said, "That's strange..." She looked up to the roof again and the silence.

"Soundproof. who knows. It looks old," said Sam stretching his legs.

Mia walked to the edge of the shelter and stared out at the rain. "They didn't forecast this. I checked before I came out." She foraged in her bag and pulled out her phone. "I can't get a signal. There is nothing." She waved the phone around. Sam looked at her.

She wasn't a bad-looking girl – brunette, natural too, and petite – just his type. He smiled. "It's the thunder. Something to do with electromagnetic energy. And I don't suppose this shelter helps. It's solid." He banged the wall with the flat of his hand. "A tank wouldn't be able to get through it."

Mia put her phone back in her handbag and moved towards the side of the shelter. She saw a timetable in a metal frame and traced her finger along the days and downwards to the times. "Wow, there's a bus at 3 a.m."

"You're kidding!"

"Straight up. Look," said Mia, retracing the timetable with her finger.

"A night bus!" Sam got up and moved closer to where Mia was pointing. "Maybe our luck hasn't run out." He looked at his watch, but the face was smashed. "Bastards! Do you have the time?"

"I can't wear watches. They go funny on me." She looked at her phone, and then tutted. "That's all I need. I think the battery has gone dead."

Sam looked down at the floor and began to pace. "Okay, I was at the bar at one-thirty then all that shit kicked off… Micky and Jay left early and…" He looked at Mia and pointed. "And you found me around two?" Mia nodded.

"Yeah, sounds about right. But… I left earlier for my cab." She frowned. "Yeah, I left early… The cab arrived at the side… I was walking and…" She looked at Sam. "I feel cold." She began shivering. He put his arm around her. "Only body warmth – no funny business."

He held up a hand. "Scout's honour." Mia stared vacantly. Sam waved his hand across her face. "Come in, Planet Mia." She blinked.

"I'm sorry, it's all a bit vague." She rubbed her head. "I don't know… I can't remember…" She looked away.

"Do you think you may have had your drink spiked?"

She looked at Sam and shook her head. "I don't know, but…" She became upset and looked down at her bare feet. "I can't remember… Everything went quiet, and then I heard something."

"And?"

"It was shouting in the distance… Yes, in the distance. Come back! Come back!" She stared blankly looking at a hazy figure. She blinked, and then it disappeared. Sam pulled her closer.

They both stood holding each other looking out of the bus shelter.

"You'll be home soon." Sam looked out at rain. "What a night. We were out celebrating my new promotion… Who would've thought…?" He looked down at Mia.

Sam looked over at the bus timetable. "It will be cheaper than a cab, a night bus." He laughed. They both watched the rain forming large puddles outside the shelter. "My folks will give me grief over the watch. It was their twenty-first birthday present to me." He looked down at his wrist. "That pig of a bouncer pushed me down the steps."

"Do you think you slipped? You looked a bit out of it?" Mia looked at him.

Sam felt his head. "No, I remember him grabbing my arm and pushing me down. The bastard pig." Mia rummaged in her handbag as Sam ranted. "He had it in for me. Jealous, that's what it was. The bastard."

Mia pulled out a small pink gauze bag, opened it, took out a tiny brightly coloured doll and placed it in her hands.

"What's that?" he asked, laughing.

"It's my protection." She held up the doll. "I always get it out when I feel blue. When I have it, I know I will be safe."

"In what way?" Sam frowned.

Stroking the doll, Mia replied, "My auntie said a shaman put some type of protection blessing on it, so no matter what happens, I will never come to any harm." She smiled looking at the brightly coloured doll.

"Let's have a look."

Mia handed him the doll. He walked over to the bulkhead light and carefully examined it.

"Is it voodoo?" He inspected the doll's face and rotated it between his fingers.

Suddenly, it shot out of his hand and flew across to the wooden bench.

"Oh no! Where's it gone?" Mia ran across. "It's fallen between the wooden slats of the seat. It's jammed in. I can see it." She pushed her fingers in the gap of the seat. "Get something to poke it out."

Sam searched around and found a twig and levelled it in between the wooden slats. "I can see it. Move away, I can't see… I need the light." Mia stood behind Sam as he attempted to reach the doll.

"She's not going to fall deeper! I can't lose her!" Mia said desperately, watching Sam stick the twig deeper between the slats. "Quick, it's falling! Please get it back!" Mia cried, upon seeing the doll slip further down.

Sam knelt down as he positioned the stick from a different angle. "I can't see it. I need more light."

Just then, a light shone directly down.

"Thanks, that's better. Yeah, it's slipped down. Oh shit, it's gone." He stood up and turned towards Mia, but she was not there.

A tall figure stood staring down at Sam.

Sam stared directly up into the amber-coloured eyes of the man.

"Can I help?" The man smiled as Sam stood staring into his eyes. Sam froze. "I'm sorry I startled you. I would like to help you." Sam took a step back. "Please let me help you. I have light." He held up his hand; it shone brightly. Sam stood staring as the man walked towards him.

"Thanks, but I think it's gone... Mia?" He looked around and saw her standing in the far corner of the bus shelter.

"Please, I would like to help you." A sweet smell filled the shelter. The man towered over Sam as if standing on tiptoe, his hand getting brighter, and just for a moment Sam thought he heard the sound of hooves moving across the concrete floor.

"No, it's just... It's late and we're..."

"Waiting for the bus. It shouldn't be too long..." The man smiled.

Sam looked over to Mia, who shook her head.

"No, it's all right. It's disappeared anyway."

The man tilted his head as he looked down at Sam. "That is a shame, and such a pretty doll." He smiled holding out his hand, which was still shining brightly.

Walking over to Mia, Sam asked, "You okay?" She nodded. "Where did he come from? I didn't hear anyone come in," he whispered.

"He just appeared," she replied. "I felt his breath on my neck and smelt the sickly-sweet smell. I feel sick…" Sam put his arm around her.

"The bus shouldn't be long," said Sam, looking over to where the man had stood. "Where's he gone?" He looked around. "Hey, mister, you there? The bus will be coming soon." He walked to the edge of the shelter and looked out to the rain still pummelling down. "You out there, mister? You'll get wet." Sam peered around the corner of the shelter. "Hey, you there?" he called before looking back at Mia.

Mia looked across at a row of old tenement flats. "He probably came from over there." She pointed. "A lot of homeless and down-and-outs live there."

Sam looked across at the torn curtains and broken blinds. "Yeah, I guess so. Strange, though." He shuddered. "I feel as if he's watching."

"Maybe we disturbed him," said Mia. "He could have been sleeping in the shelter."

"There was no one here, Mia. He just appeared."

Mia looked at Sam and nodded. "He wasn't wet".

Looking out at the rain, Sam said, "This place is weird. I just want to go home… I'm tired." They both stood at the edge of the shelter. "We can make a run for it?" Sam looked at Mia.

Another loud thunderclap crashed overhead. Mia screamed. The lightning continued to light up the sky, flashing overhead, followed by a further crash.

"Rain, rain, go away. Come back another day," Mia kept repeating.

Sam pulled her closer. "Don't worry, the bus will be here soon. We'll be safe then." He felt her warmth as she clung to him.

The sound of rock music filled the shelter. Sam looked around and saw a tall guy sitting on the seat, his head tilting towards the wall as he moved in time to the beat of the music.

"Look." Mia tugged Sam's shirt.

A woman walked towards them pushing a pram. Sam heard talking and laughing and saw a group of five lads. One of them jumped and grabbed the lip of the guttering on the shelter roof and began doing pull-ups. Another counted each time he pulled his chin up.

"The bus must be coming soon." Mia wiped her tears and smiled.

Sam watched a young couple run down the street.

"Bloody rain. Has the night bus left yet?" asked the man.

"No, mate." Sam looked down at Mia. "You see, it's going to be all right."

Mia looked at the couple and watched them standing in the shelter.

The girl shook the rain from her jacket and looked at the man. "You see, I was right," she said. Admiring the ring on her finger, she said, "It's beautiful," and then looked up at the man and kissed him. "You're stuck with me forever."

The rain continued as Sam and Mia stood at the edge of the bus shelter.

"It must be here soon," said Mia.

Sam looked at Mia resting her head against his shoulder; he could see that she was tired. He smiled and whispered into her ear, "Hey you, would you like to go out next week?" Mia looked up, her eyes half closed. She smiled and nodded.

"I'd like that."

He kissed her forehead. "Here's the big ask. What's your number?"

Rummaging in her bag, "I've got a pen." She continued to rustle around and pulled out a black eyeliner and handed it to Sam. He looked at it. "Take the top off. It should be pointed enough to write." She called out her number. "No five – you've written three."

Sam traced over the number on his hand and read it out again to double-check. "I hope it's waterproof."

"Yeah, of course it is. Look at my eyes." Mia laughed.

Sam bent forward and kissed her.

The guys behind clapped and roared with laughter. Sam looked over at the group of lads.

"Two hundred." They continued laughing and clapping as their friend struggled to do the final pull-up.

"It's coming!" the woman with the pushchair announced.

Mia clung to Sam and watched a red double decker bus emerge from around the corner moving slowly towards the bus shelter.

"I've just thought, do we need the exact change?" Sam looked at Mia.

"I don't know. I may have some in here." She searched through her handbag.

"Here, this should be enough." The young guy listening to music passed Sam a five-pound note.

"Thanks, mate. I'll pay you back". He looked at the youth, who nodded and looked away.

The smell of diesel filled the air as the bus stopped directly outside the shelter. Sam pulled Mia to one side as he let the woman with the pushchair go before them.

"We may as well let the others on first to see where they sit, and then we can be alone." He looked at Mia and winked. She blushed.

The group of lads got on chanting and headed for the top of the bus. The young couple followed behind and sat at the front of the top deck. The young guy listening to music paused and looked back towards Mia. He had a smooth white complexion and red cheeks. She smiled as he looked down at the ground and slowly climbed the steps.

"We'd better get on. We don't want to be stuck here…" Sam hopped onto the steps. "I'll get us a seat at the back on the lower deck."

Mia was about to place her foot on the step when she heard a voice.

"Excuse me, miss. I think this belongs to you."

Turning around, Mia saw the tall man standing in the shelter. He was holding the brightly coloured doll. She ran over.

"Oh, thank you! You don't know how much this means! Thank you so much." The man placed the doll in the centre of her palm. Mia went to look up at the man, but he was gone. She clutched the doll tightly and kissed it. "Thank you."

The bus engine roared as the doors closed.

Mia turned. "No! Wait! Please wait!" She ran towards the bus. "Stop! Please stop! Sam, make the bus stop! Sam!" she screamed. She watched Sam looking out of the back of the bus. He placed his palm against the window. "Sam, stop the bus!" she cried. "Please stop! I want to go home. I must get home… Please!" She stood in the middle of the street as the bus disappeared.

Suddenly, shards of light cut through as a hazy figure stood over her.

"Come back! Come back!"

The light became brighter.

"Her eyes, they're opening. Make her comfortable. Cover her legs with something and give her more air. We need to get her stabilised."

"Hello! Are you okay?" a man's voice shouted.

A woman with crimped hair and large earrings knelt down. "I was so worried about you. I saw…" She broke off. "It wasn't your time," she whispered.

The paramedic looked down while running more checks on her. Two policeman stood watching.

"This is the worst night of my life. We've had the minibus crash from some society, PENDA or some group of middle-aged misfits, the five football supporters in a car, which collided with another couple, and they're all dead." The policeman shook his head. "We've received reports of a man being seen on the central reservation wearing a green waistcoat, but he's not amongst the dead." He took a deep breath. "This is hell. And a suicide!" He turned his face to wipe away a tear. "A young lad. He was twenty-six years old and had so much to live for. He died listening to his rock music." His hands trembled while continuing to write in his notebook. "And the woman with a pram, knocked down – another hit-and-run – and now this…" He looked at Mia. "Do you think she'll remember much?"

"We've picked up the cab driver… We've ran checks, but he wasn't registered," said another police officer.

The policeman looked down at his notepad. "The young lad at the front of the night club… He's dead… The door staff are being questioned." He paused. "He has a number on his hand. I'll call it." He shook his head again as he began to dial the number. "What a night."

Mia lay on the stretcher gazing up at the night sky as she was put into the back of the ambulance. She clutched the doll tightly as her mobile phone began to ring…

Ink Blot

No one can quite remember when it all happened, but whoever was responsible for the strange events was an outsider, and their presence destroyed the tranquillity of the village which would never return. One local described the events of the summer of 2016 as though "a dark ink blot had descended on the whole village".

It was the Michaelmas term of 2016 when it all started. A maroon-coloured Citroën 2CV appeared, advertising a new enterprise. Its occupant, a female, drove down the narrow streets with long bitumen-black hair and wore the most intense blue eye shadow. The police knew her name as Tulpa, and her shop Abracadabra was quirky with resin skulls, amulets and stuffed animals. Many thought her a taxidermist, but she described herself as an artist who specialised in skin motifs. The shop, which occupied one of the boarded-up banks, kept unusual opening hours; and if anyone ventured past, they would be met with a sweet, lingering aroma and singing, described by many as mesmerising and overpowering.

Little was known about Tulpa, other than she'd trained in fine art and had an accent which was described as a mixture of American or Canadian with a lilt of either French or Italian.

One of the police reports noted that she may have had connections in the area, although upon further enquiries no evidence of this could be found. There was a consensus that the shop walls were covered with unusual art. "She was talented and her pictures so realistic; I felt I'd been transported back in time," one local was recorded as saying.

Initially, Tulpa was met with intrigue. The shop was interesting, and the local gossips walked by to inspect. One nodded towards it saying, "Hardly in keeping with the village – and the name, is she a magician?" There were scoffs of laughter.

"Perhaps a bistro or artisan baker would have been better," someone else suggested.

After a few weeks, the people became accustomed to Abracadabra and the sight of Tulpa in the high street wearing a long black flowing dress with a teal scarf undulating in the breeze. She soon blended into the community.

Each Wednesday, a flock of corporate wives descended upon the village to catch up on the latest news and their children's after-school activities.

"I've got Sam in the regional final of chess, and he's doing well at the flute too. I've booked him in for more lessons. Penny is excelling at the clarinet, but I need her to improve, so I've increased her lessons," Della said while running through her itinerary.

"I've increased Melody's violin lessons, and she's doing drama and voice projection. Let's see, every Tuesday, Wednesday and Friday." Greta swiped through her phone. "I may put her name down for one of those community projects."

Looking through her phone, Bellini said, "Zeb is in the cross-country finals, and he's doing well in the school orchestra. I'll have to put him in for some extra lessons along with Laura and Milly." She winced. "Strings, darling. They do try, and I think they're coming on leaps and bounds."

Tara checked her phone as she rescheduled one of her charity events. "Nina is doing well at the piano, but I want to be on the safe side, so I've booked her in for another lesson. And I've put her down for some more after-school clubs. I need to max out her extracurricular activities otherwise the new school won't take her."

Della looked up and cleared her voice as they moved on to their main topic of conversation: Marcus.

He was the new personal trainer at the gym. He'd come highly recommended, and all the corporate wives had booked him for their personal one-to-one sessions.

"He oozes masculinity. And his arms – they are so strong. And the size of his hands." Della sighed rolling her neck.

They looked at each other and sniggered.

"It's the body art that intrigues me," Greta said, staring into her cappuccino. She looked up and licked her spoon. They all nodded at each other. Marcus had the most unusual colourful body art.

Bellini remarked, "When I had a sesh with him—" The others began laughing. "Personal training, darlings... He held my feet, lifting them off the floor, and I saw two huge eyes similar to an owl staring at me from the tattoos on each arm. They looked right through me." Two of the women stared at her.

"You need to hydrate yourself more," Della suggested.

"I remember when he was massaging my neck, I felt the smoothness of fur and heard the purring of a cat," Greta added, rolling her head from side to side.

They all agreed that Marcus was something special.

"Oh, how the mind plays tricks – especially when you're in a high state of *arousal*." They all laughed as Bellini lingered over the last word.

"I was thinking of getting a tattoo," said Tara, clearing her throat. "Nothing too gauche. Just a simple design, perhaps the children's initials, certainly no bigger than a ten-pence piece." The women looked at each other.

"Yes, I'd like one." Della, Greta, Tara and Bellini placed their hands on each other's and agreed.

"But where does one acquire such a thing?" Della asked.

They all looked across in the direction of Abracadabra and at Tulpa standing outside organising a new window display.

The bell echoed when Greta entered Abracadabra. She stood looking at the blood-red walls, the white panelling and two stuffed crows perched on a branch hanging in the corner. She was about to turn when she heard singing. Looking around, she saw the most beautiful picture of a meadow on the far side of the wall. It appeared as though someone had opened a window.

She walked closer and found herself transported into the middle of the meadow, wearing a white flowing dress and surrounded by blue cornflowers, poppies, daisies and meadowsweet. The aroma was soporific as she walked barefoot. She could hear birds – a thrush, a blackbird and a warbler hovering nearby. Feeling very tired, she lay down looking up at the sky watching the birds fly overhead. She could see patterns forming and felt a warmth travelling through her body, which made her sink further into a deep state of relaxation. A dove landed next to her, and then a burst of white light rushed out through the crown of her head, which caused her to jolt.

A while later, Greta awoke. Focusing her eyes, she found herself lying on the sofa in her lounge. She looked at the clock and heard a voice.

"Sleeping beauty has arisen. Will you be joining us for dinner?" Tim, her husband, asked as he poked his head around the door.

Greta stretched and as she did so, she felt a tingling at the top of her arm. It was then she noticed the tattoo of poppies, a violin and the letter "M".

Della picked up the fabric for her curtains. She'd decided on muted tones for the decoration which Tariq, her husband, and her two children, Sammy and Penny, approved of. Before heading back, she decided to walk past Abracadabra – more out of curiosity, as Greta hadn't reported back to the clan yet about her experience because Tim had sprung a last-minute getaway to visit his family in Betws-y-Coed.

As Della stood peering through the door, a tall dark man with a beard rushed out and began punching the air around him, as though trying to fight someone. She watched him disappear down a narrow street.

Turning to go into Tulpa's shop, she thought just for a moment that she could hear a roaring lion. She looked around and found herself standing in the middle of the shop, surrounded by walls painted Prussian blue, with gold paint covering the picture rails and door trims. She was going to go towards the door, but the sound of the sea drew her over to a mural on the far side.

She walked closer and felt herself walking along a beach. She could feel the warm sand under her feet and the breeze through her red hair. She looked out across the sea and the changes of colour as it rippled from azure to turquoise. She walked to the edge of the shore and felt the sea wash over her feet and the gentle pull as she looked across at a small boat and a man waving. Della waved back laughing and as she walked further into the sea, she felt someone tap her shoulder.

"I'm sorry. Can I pass?" an older woman asked, pushing a pram.

Della was now standing on the high street gazing into the estate agent's window. She felt a scratch on her arm. Lifting her blouse exposed a small tattoo of a mermaid and the letters "P" and "S" intertwined with a flute and clarinet.

Tara had been out of town on an errand for her daughter, Nina, who was sitting her grade six piano exam. She wanted to buy her something special, perhaps a good luck charm, so thought about a bracelet. She found an amber and silver one which was in keeping with her daughter's minimalistic look.

But as she drove through Braydene, she remembered that her husband wanted a single malt from the local vintners. She parked in the short-stay car park and hurried along the high street, finding herself in front of Abracadabra. It was closed.

Walking further up the high street, Tara found herself in a department store filled with the most beautiful furniture. She browsed and found a chaise longue in dusky pink. It was something she'd always wanted, and it was only last week that she'd dropped a hint about it to her husband and Nina when discussing her fiftieth birthday.

She felt the soft fabric, slipped off her shoes and sat down swinging her legs around. It felt so comfortable, and the colour would go well in the bedroom. She heard the singing and laughter of children, and smiled as she drifted deeper with a warmth filling her body.

Then there was a loud cough. Tara opened her eyes and looked directly ahead at a park attendant and an empty bottle of whiskey at her feet. She hurried away and felt a pulling at the top of her arm, where she saw a tattoo with the initial "N" etched with two piano keys.

Bellini sat looking at herself in the mirror. Her eleven o'clock appointment hadn't turned up, and her next one wasn't until three. She reapplied her make-up and lip gloss and after tidying up her desk decided to go for a walk.

She enjoyed being a financial advisor. Organising other people's finances gave her a valuable insight into people's behaviour, and she was adept at spotting anomalies, such as those snatched weekends away and gifts of perfume and lingerie where the wife was strangely absent. Her keen eye for detail earnt her extra perks, which kept her three children, Zeb, Laura and Milly, in a good lifestyle. They all attended private school and excelled in their extracurricular activities, and she was especially proud of their accomplishments in the youth orchestra. She had a good life, and her children didn't want for anything.

She pottered down the high street thinking of what to have for lunch. Bellini liked her food and often decried how nature had been cruel by making her big-boned.

As she headed in search of goodies, she saw Greta cut down one of the side streets. She quickened her pace and called after her friend as she saw her leopard-print shoes enter Abracadabra. Bellini followed, and then found herself in the middle of a forest. She could smell cedar wood burning, and there was a small hut in the distance and a campfire. Taking a deep breath, she could smell the succulent aroma of roast pork as the crackling sizzled under the heat of raw flames. How she loved a pork sandwich with lashings of apple.

She approached the food and looked around. There was no one there. She sat down, took the knife and began carving chunks of the pork and placed it inside two huge slices of rustic bread. The meat melted in her mouth – and the apple sauce, so sweet and fresh as though the fruit had just been picked. She cut more meat and bread and as she shovelled it back, she made a mental note to phone the gym and book Marcus for two double sessions, which she hoped would prevent the fat from circumventing her spare tyres.

Feeling very tired, she lay down on a blanket next to the fire. Two carrion crows looked down as she dropped off to sleep. A gentle hum filled the air while she drifted deeper and a warm feeling travelled through her body, followed by a white light that circulated above her head.

Suddenly, she felt a pinch on her shoulder which woke her, and she found a seagull jabbing its beak at her sandwich. Flailing her arms around, she now realised she was standing on the village green, and it was then that she saw the small tattoo at the top of her right arm with the initials "Z", "L" and "M" circled with a violin and cello.

Two weeks later, the women met up and compared their respective tattoos.

"I don't actually remember having mine," Tara said, inspecting the others.

"Strange you mention that…" Greta said, stroking the mermaid on Della's arm.

"I can't remember choosing my design," said Bellini. "But I must have done…" They all nodded.

"I can't remember having a discussion with Tulpa." Greta looked at Bellini who agreed.

Tara leant forward. "I see Marcus has another tattoo. I saw it when he bent down. It must go all the way down."

"All the way down?" Greta blushed.

Tara nodded as Bellini's eyes widened. "I am booking more sessions." The women looked at each other.

"I was thinking along the same lines, too, dear," Bellini said as she began texting Marcus.

Della and Greta laughed.

"I make sure he sees my tattoo." Tara sat looking at her body art. "It's so lifelike. I can almost hear Nina playing the piano."

"Yes, I hear the strings." Bellini laughed, before dolloping another spoon of Chantilly cream on her apple slice.

"Isn't that bizarre – I can hear the clarinet and flute," said Della.

They all laughed as they arranged a night out.

"I'm sure Marcus lives that way. We may bump into him." Tara winked.

It must have been several weeks into the Trinity term that strange things began to happen. They were subtle at first, such as a couple of cats going missing.

"Someone is feeding them. Cats are so fickle. You're as good as your last meal with those wretched creatures," Bellini scoffed as one of her clients mentioned it while filling in a new mortgage application.

A couple of the shops had closed on the high street. "Sadly, a sign of the times," Greta remarked when they met up. "I've increased my one-to-one sessions with Marcus. I don't want him to feel that we've let him down." The others nodded in agreement.

"Tariq doesn't seem concerned about the local economy. He mentioned that his company has won another multimillion-pound deal," Della said as she ordered another cream cake.

"That's what Tim said." Greta reached for an almond slice.

"Haydn too. He'll be travelling more," Tara said, nodding in agreement.

"My firm is expanding and want me to take on another office." Bellini laughed.

Tara looked across the table at them. "There's a recession going on around us, and we're reaping the benefits. I feel as though we've been compensated for something."

Greta nodded. "The common denominator is Marcus." They all laughed.

"It's down to sheer hard work and all the money we raise. We should get a gong next," Della said as she cut another slice of the apple tart. "Talking of which, it's the school prom in a fortnight." They all looked at each other.

"Goodness, I'd forgotten," Greta said, glancing at the others.

"It's a huge extravaganza, and all the children and their wretched teachers are going on about it. Organised by some foreign-sounding bloke…" Della said, passing the slice of apple tart to Bellini.

They all looked at their schedules.

"I can't make it," Tara announced, scrolling across the calendar on her mobile.

"Me neither," Greta added, fumbling through her phone.

"What a calamity. What are we going to do?" mumbled Bellini as she shoved the last morsels of apple pie into her mouth.

They all turned to Della.

"Would you mind, darling, if I dropped Melody off at yours?" Greta asked as she refilled her cup. "There's a coach, and the poppets so do want to go on it."

"Yes, could we all be such pains and drop the sprogs off at yours, Della, dear? I know Zeb, Laura and Milly will be late if I don't," Bellini said while texting.

"Yes, darling, can I drop off Nina?" Tara asked, stroking Della's arm.

They all agreed the children would be dropped off at Della's. Each one of them would do an errand for Della in return.

"This is on me. I can put it through the business account." Bellini stood up. "This orchestral thingamabob, who's organising it again?"

They all looked at each other and shrugged.

"I can't remember his name now… And I understand Tulpa is helping out," Della said.

They all looked out across to Abracadabra.

"Face painting, I expect," Tara said, looking over her glasses. They all laughed.

Two weeks later, everyone descended at Della's. She'd arranged for the bus company to pick up the children from the front of her house.

"Single file, please!" Della shouted, waving a typed-up itinerary.

The children queued carrying their various musical instruments. She started off with her own children.

"Sammy and Penny." She smiled marking them off and gave each one a big kiss. "You won't let Mummy down will you?" They both looked at each other and smirked before climbing onto the bus. "It's all so exciting, isn't it, Zeb, Laura and Milly?" She crossed them off the list. "The best of luck to you all." She nodded. "Please leave your instruments by here. I'll get the driver to store them under here." She tapped the side of the bus with her hand. "Melody, dear, please don't do that. There's a good girl." Della ushered her onto the bus. "There you go." Nina wheeled her keyboard to the front of the bus. "Driver, please be a dear and store it carefully along with these." Della checked Nina off her list.

The bus driver stood watching. He walked over to the side of the bus and opened up the luggage door.

Della popped on board, walked down the aisle and counted everyone. "We have a few others too. Patrick, Tilly, Angharad, Jacob, Celia and Sita." Each raised their hand. "Goodness, that's thirteen – unlucky for some." She chuckled. Della then turned around and saw the bus driver staring out through the windscreen. As she walked over to him, a cold gust of air blew her back. "Please turn the air con off. It isn't good for them." She moved closer to him. "I thought I told you to store away the musical instruments."

He turned his head slowly and looked at her. He had dark eyes and his complexion was pale. "I have done as you requested, madam," he said slowly. He faced forward again and started the engine.

Della mumbled something under her breath, and then turned back to the children. "Remember to text your mummies upon arrival, and may the best boy or girl win." She pointed to Sammy and Penny.

All the children sat looking at their phones. Della climbed off the bus and watched as it travelled down the long drive. She walked halfway and saw a maroon car follow with two occupants inside…

"His eyes were so deep. Yes, a deep blue or … green? Whatever colour they were… I'd notice him again. He had an illuminous glow. Yes, he was strange, and the bag he had. A leather bag, which he kept his paperwork in near the dashboard. Similar to the one the doctor used to carry." Della began crying. "If only I'd stopped him. His name, yes, strange, double-barrelled, I think… Dominic van Sant. He said he only collected. I didn't know what he meant at the time… but …" Della wailed giving her statement.

"And Tulpa, do you know anything about her?" asked the young police officer.

Della shook her head. "She vanished – and her shop, as though it didn't exist."

"We're trying to trace a number of people… Do you know Marcus…?" The police officer flipped through his notebook.

"Just someone in the gym." Della looked at him, tears rolling down her face. "He's vanished, too.

Everything has gone. All the children, and Marcus. I have nothing." She knelt down on the gravel crying. "And the music – all I can hear is the flute and clarinet." She sobbed holding her hands to the side of her head. "I can't stand it anymore."

The police officer ushered over a female colleague to comfort her. He then got into his car and drove down the tree-lined drive, away from the five-bedroomed house and to the major incident room, which had been set up in the town centre to investigate the disappearance of the thirteen children.

On the way, he stopped by one of the local housing estates and watched the children swing on a rope attached to a tree, balance on a makeshift climbing frame and run around playing with each other, with their parents looking on.

The End

www.ingramcontent.com/pod-product-compliance
Lightning Source LLC
Chambersburg PA
CBHW031103080526
44587CB00011B/805